Making Space to Breathe

Journeys with Johnna

Making Space to Breathe

CONTENTS

Introduction

As we begin on the path of healing trauma, whether in this lifetime, past lives, or within your generational lineage, you quickly learn that your intuition will lead you in some pretty wild directions. When I first began my emotional and spiritual healing journey, it was in therapy over ten years ago, at this time, I didn't really understand the concept of intuition. Though I'd been encouraged to follow intuition as a child and all growing up, I think my mom was the only person I knew doing this and teaching it. Of course, at that age, the last thing we want to do is what our mom tells us. So I pushed this idea so far away from myself that when my therapist was teaching me the concept, I couldn't even recognize it.

Fast forward years later and I cannot image living my life not being led by my intuition. The more I heal my life, the more connected I become to myself, then the more easily I am able to follow my intuition. I've gone from barely understanding the word, "intuition", to walking by faith most days...which is where we meet one another in this book. I was following my intuition so blindly that it took me to live on the other side of the world, multiple times over the recent years. I didn't know that following these nudges would lead me to the greatest journey, to date, in my life. The journey to heal emotional abuse that permeated my existence.

When I was first called to live in Bali in 2019, I broke down crying. I'd only just arrived in Bali and had been on the island for less than three weeks when a message came through so powerful that I couldn't ignore it. Through meditation class in my Yoga Teacher Training (YTT), a voice said, "You belong here, you're home, stay and heal." I cried on the shoulder of my other American friend who'd left to travel through Asia for a few months, eight months prior to me meeting her...she said, "I get it, I'm not going back either."

Thoughts were reeling in my head, "How can I leave my family? They'll be so mad at me! How will I support myself?" All these thoughts just kept getting the same answer over the coming weeks, "It will all work out, trust the process."

I left Bali a month later to meet with a travel group that was going to travel through Asia, beginning in Vietnam. I almost canceled the trip and would have, had the group not been meeting in Vietnam. As I felt strongly I needed to be in that country. My father and several Uncles are War Veterans of the American - -Vietnam War. When I told my parents I was taking off for six months to travel through Asia, my dad was a little excited, he'd always spoken very highly of Asia and it's people. He replied, "Okay, just don't go to Vietnam". I explained it was the 2nd country I would live in, he was visibly upset. I knew I needed to be in Vietnam to help clear karma from his experience there that resided within my body.

At the time of this trip, it was early 2019, and I hadn't done any studying or reading on karma, Quantum Psychics, past lives, DNA memory...I didn't know any of this on a spiritual or scientific level. I was following my intuition and spirit guides who told me to go. Vietnam was the first country that I intentionally slowed down in to observe my surroundings and to come back to myself. As my group drove through the countryside and took an overnight train to hike Sa Pa, go boating through Ha Long Bay, or lay beachside in Hoi An, I could feel something releasing from my body. I could feel anxiety and fear of the world leaving as I took in this country that my father lived in through one of its most gruesome historical events.

While in Vietnam, I lived in Hanoi, a large, polluted, loud as fuck city that quickly overwhelmed me as these emotions were released. With thousands of people driving their scooters so rapidly through the city, I needed help across the streets like a small child. As new friends were compassionate enough to hold my hand to escort me across, I'd never felt so much crippling anxiety before or since. As I've learned throughout my healing journey when you're healing something specific, like I was working on my anxiety, it gets worse before it gets better...the anxiety needs to come up to come out. So while I lived in this loud city, learning to release, work with, and not shame my anxiety, some days it was worse before it was better.

One night I did a cord-clearing ritual for myself to Vietnam, clearing the pain that this country had put in my DNA and sending it back to the land. I felt relieved, much better than I had the previous few weeks of living here. I was refreshed after all our trips to the smaller more quiet places that house delicious Vietnamese food and the sweetest group of people. I loved the culture and following the ritual, I felt so much peace that I considered moving to Hoi An, though quickly realized that wasn't the right place for me.

My travel group and I then traveled to Thailand, where the sun was shining, my spirits were lifted, and a community of Buddhists who were so welcoming anywhere you went. I loved hearing the Thai people drive by on their scooters laughing, and not honking horns in the city of Chang Mai because they found it rude. Unlike the busyness of Hanoi, Chang Mai was more laid back, people slowed down when you crossed the street and smiled as you went by. I felt welcomed and comfortable in this country. One where I could've easily lived, had I been called to do so.

Thailand gave me that gumption of self-exploration for myself and for life that I needed! It taught me to find the balance and to remain true to my spiritual gifts.

Next, we flew to Japan, where my creative side was able to blossom. Living in the smaller city of Kyoto, riding my gold cruiser bicycle, which I called Marigold, and eating sushi like it was going out of style. The fashion completely opened me up to something more creative, passed what I'd been wearing most of my life in Texas, with the exception of my weird teenage years. Pairing patterns with patterns, neon's with furs, and pearls with boots, plus everything in between...the fashion in Japan let me see and accept that my creativity was something to be proud of and not ashamed of...knowing that my current career choice of real estate wasn't the right path for me but that something in the arts was. I felt I was able to totally breathe easily in Japan because it was quiet...from the immaculately manicured Zen gardens to learning about Reiki, to getting fortunes from a temple that I still carry with me today, I loved this country. I could see myself in a whole new life here. If I moved there when I was twenty years old it probably would've worked out, but now it wasn't for me. It did however let me fall completely in love with myself and all that I have to offer.

Next on the list was Malaysia...living in Kuala Lumpur wasn't my cup of tea with the exception of the amazing food! This one allowed me to open up and really appreciate cuisine from around the world, and where I welcomed in solitude. In this solitude, I could see and accept that I had a purpose in teaching others through my experiences, showing people how to slow down and how to accept themselves. A seed was planted in the solitude of Kuala Lumpur, one that would take a few more years to grow.

Following Malaysia, I was called to go back to Bali. I stayed somewhere new this time and looked at it differently, everywhere I went, everyone I encountered was from the lens of living here rather than as a tourist. During this trip to Bali, the message came back again, "Don't leave stay here to heal." I felt I couldn't do this though. I think my friends and family could feel the same as I was receiving more and more frequent calls and reminders that it was time to go back to Texas, by their standards. I reluctantly booked my ticket back to the

States, and that same night I booked a ticket out of the States to explore Europe.

Bali on the other hand had another idea…a few nights before I was to leave my grandfather died, one who I hadn't gotten along with much but one who played a huge role in my life. I grieved his death for my grandmother, they'd been married for over seventy years at his passing. She'd been at his side since they were children. I loved my grandmother and grieved for the loss I could only imagine she was feeling. As I looked in the mirror that night the message came to me more clearly…

"Stay here to heal. Heal the emotionally abusive pattern that you've been in."

I debated canceling my flight but I didn't, I felt that despite this message I needed to go home to see my family. It took me over four days to get home, missing the funeral. My flights leaving Bali were canceled and rescheduled twice. I was not supposed to be leaving at that time… since I chose differently, another path opened up for me.

I went back to the States and began to sell my belongings and make peace with my decision to move to Bali. I went to Europe to teach yoga and live in Tenerife where I met a man who'd become a wonderful friend for me. He could see that I was struggling physically and had been sick for most of my life, pushing through and doing my best when my best was operating at about 45%-55% most days. I look back at this and wonder just how I worked 50+ hours per week and also had energy for a social life at the bars.

I had planned to go directly back to the States, finish selling my things, and go to Bali when we met. However, the Universe had other plans. Together with my new boyfriend, we decided to travel to India to do Panchakarma, healing the body on a deep level of toxins and disease. Six weeks before we were supposed to head to India, we got an email from the retreat space in Kerala that they needed to push back our trip. On the same day, a tenant living in his flat in Amsterdam said he was let go from his job and was moving back to Australia within a week. We saw it as a sign and both moved back to Amsterdam together...we were still set to go to India and three days before we were going to travel, the world went into a global lockdown and our flights were cancelled. Furious with the process, I wanted to be in India and then go back to Bali! We stayed put in Amsterdam, to live in a busy city that was all of a sudden very quiet and empty.

I took this opportunity to slow down even more, to take time for rest, and to work on my health in a way I'd never done before. I didn't know it at the time but in order for me to get back to Bali, I was going to need my strength for what was coming. After living in Amsterdam for six months I went back to the States as Bali was closed. I finished what I'd started, selling everything I owed, down to a few boxes stored at my parents...and waited for Bali to open.

In this waiting period, I rested, I had closed my real estate business, sold all my possessions, and quit drinking alcohol for the first time in my life. Newly sober I was navigating a whole new world. I received messages from my spirit guides that I'd be in Bali for two years doing very powerful work and a lot of healing. I had built up in my head what that would look like and living on the island was nothing of what I'd envisioned.

To be honest I was partly annoyed that I was being called so strongly to go live in Bali. Partly because I wasn't that excited about being so far from family and another part because Bali is really loud. In my time living in Amsterdam during a lockdown, it was so quiet and peaceful. I'd sit in my fourth-floor window watching the world go by, beautiful green and yellow Parrots in the trees, (yes parrots) with orange beaks who'd I get so excited to see! Cats in almost every window, all of us wearing a fashionable thrifted sweater...I'd learned to really slow down and to take in my surroundings. I'd learned that cities were absolutely not for me, something I already knew but living in a European city finalized that inner knowing for me. I concluded that I didn't like loud noises, bright lights, or for that matter a lot of people around.

I deeply desired to live way in nature and have my own garden, all the pets and friends visiting from time to time. Bali has been anything but that! While I wasn't as thrilled about it, I still moved to the island because the calling for me was so loud I couldn't ignore it unless I wanted to start drinking again or distract myself from what my spirit was saying. So I arrived during a global lockdown, on to an island that was looking at the outside world like it was mad...I had put myself into a bubble, a healing cocoon that lasted two years, and two months.

Upon arrival I immediately began my healing journey, I found a Traditional Chinese Medicine Practitioner, who regulated my irregular heartbeat and advised me to sleep for six months, this I did. Through acupuncture, energy work, herbs, and loving mentorship he was able to get my mind, body & spirit into alignment to be fearless in following my intuition. If there's one thing that all of my travels have taught me it's the powerful connection of the mind, body & spirit. Plus the amount of time and effort it takes to nurture and align these for better health overall.

I began writing a book during my downtime, but it wasn't yet ready to come out. So I knew one day that it would and that was part of why I came to Bali. I have lived on this island of karma, where many people have flocked to for decades while on healing journeys. An island that is a powerful vortex for this healing, connecting to Spirit, and getting your shit together. She is an island that invites individuals to come to for a certain amount of time to heal karmic patterns and to slow down. Each person has a vastly different experience but each one walks away knowing themselves and where they're going more clearly.

Living in Bali is almost indescribable, manifestation becomes a way of living...not in the form of the way many spiritual teachers teach it but in the way of aligning the vibration of the body or the broadcast that you're sending out. You can see this is how every land operates but we are too busy to see it. You think of something and within minutes it happens...so you learn to be careful with your thoughts and words, to fully understand the power that they hold. You see that you have the ability to heal yourself in ways you never thought possible...many are called to this island for a specific reason and when that reason is over, you can choose to re-commit or to move on to something different.

Living here and clearing the emotionally abusive karmic pattern is one of the many reasons I was called to be here. I'm grateful to myself every day for following that intuition, for taking the time, for trusting the process, and for being okay in solitude so that I can learn to love myself even more than I learned in Japan.

In the healing journey we learn by working through patterns that in order to not remain in the cycle, you have to choose to be bigger than the environment that you're in. Many around you might not understand or begin doing work on themselves, that's their choice...you are bold to make the first move to create those radical changes within yourself. When I embarked on all of my travel journeys people around me in Texas were confused or not fully understand the calling, I learned to accept this because I barely understood it, I needed to live it first.

As you learn more within this book to my reasons of being called to Bali to heal, you will also learn many things about yourself. We are called to clear certain karmic relationships, emotional and abusive patterns are dominant in our society, as a global whole. This is a conversation that I've had on repeat with both men and women throughout the past decade or more. When you decide that you've had enough is when you decide to make the changes, to do the work, to fly across the globe, to sell everything they own in order to save the soul.

It begins with you.

After all, you're here for you! You're reading this book to begin to understand how you can heal from a narcissistic, emotionally abusive relationship or divorce from a narcissist.

It is your responsibility as a human on this planet to take ownership of yourself, for your life, your words, your actions, your projections, your traumas or triggers, your health, how you love and give back. This is something only you can do, no one else. When we begin to heal, we start to remove the blame placed on others for our circumstances and get brave to hold a mirror back to ourselves.

You will begin to see where boundaries need to be in place, where your voice needs to be used, where you learned certain behaviors within yourself, or why you accept certain behaviors in others. These are some things that will be shifted within the healing process so that you no longer repeat the pattern and remove yourself from the loop.

At first, this is really hard and painful, I won't lie to you and say it's easy as pie, because if it were, then everyone would be doing it right? So when something is more challenging, then fewer people do it and it becomes the path of the determined, the strong, and the brave.

This is you, strong and brave.

If you've ever doubted yourself, then I'm telling you right here and now, find a way to stop it! You're here to do a level of work that you perhaps haven't done before or have and need a fresh perspective. Either way, any work you do helps, the deeper you go helps.

In my own experience, I don't think I would've ever reached this level if I had not left home to travel the globe and clear karma across each country I lived in. Time on this planet is short and sweet, doing the work to come to love yourself, be compassionate, and find peace is definitely work that I want to do while I'm here. What about you?

As you read this book, I pray that my story and experience will help you to heal from some of your stories and experiences. I pray that you come to a place of deep self-love and an inner knowing of your worth despite the external circumstances that got you here or traumas that you've experienced. Know that you are worthy of love and worthy of so much peace...worthy of a way of being that many of us cannot even fathom.

I'd like to encourage you to give yourself some gratitude of thanks for opening this guidebook and doing the work that's laid out inside. I thank you and am honored that you chose this book to work through.

May your journey be as bold, wild, and beautiful as mine as led me to experience.

~ Johnna

1

What is Karma & Why Clear it Out

The saying goes...."Karma is a bitch." This is the narrative that we know, something you often say to someone who's wronged you, shamed you, or pissed you off... When you just want another to "get theirs", but you don't want to be the one to do it, because that's frowned upon, so we just say, "KARMA IS A BITCH!" Almost as if in the form of an energetic curse or hex.

But is karma a bitch? How are we able to make such a bold statement about something so deeply spiritual without fully understanding what it is we are saying? Or without having a full understanding of what karma actually is and how it affects each and every one of us on the planet.

So, what is Karma?

Karma - in Sanskrit (the ancient language of India) means action, work, or deed, and its effect or consequence. *

According to Buddhist and Hindu beliefs, karma is the sum of a person's actions either in this existence or in previous states of existence. ** In other words, the actions that you take in this lifetime or in a past lifetime, effects one another until these actions are cleared.

In my travels, I have lived a short time in Thailand, where many people are followers of the Buddhist philosophy and as I currently reside in Bali, many people are followers of Balinese Hinduism. Both of these geographic locations and the people who inhabit these lands are dedicated to the practice and belief of karma.

During my time in Thailand, I was introduced and began to open up to a greater understanding of this practice, by sitting down with a Buddhist Monk who was teaching myself and others about Buddhism. Explaining to us that contrary to popular belief, Buddhism is not a religion but a philosophy of how to live life, how to find balance and happiness within this lifetime that sometimes is a total mess. He told us that no matter who we are, where we come from, or what we do in life, the desire in all of us is to be happy.

Is this true for you? If you sit back to examine yourself, is one of your main desires in life to be happy? Are you happy with your life as it is at this moment? Many of us believe we are happy, without understanding our own karma or programming to be able to wholeheartedly answer this question.

The Monk proceeded to explain to us that in life we can find happiness by finding the BALANCE in life. We are only able to truly find the balance in life if we are self-aware of our thoughts, feelings, actions, and karmic patterns and how those play a role in our lives. When we are more self-aware we are more able to find the balance, clear our karma, and become more happy.

I listened to this Monk, for over one hour. I was wearing a T-shirt that said, "BALANCE." I'll never forget him making eye contact with me, pointing at my shirt, and saying, "You get it, or you wouldn't have bought or worn that shirt if you didn't subconsciously understand the importance of balance and its role in your happiness."

Tears began to roll down my face for the rest of the discussion as I absorbed every word that floated from the vibration of his voice. I felt this was a conversation that would forever change my life, and it did...I have never forgotten that hour of my life. The impact was so deep that within a 24-hour period, I took an impromptu trip to the tattoo shop to tattoo the word, "BALANCE" on my forearm...so that I would see it, be reminded, and come back to a space of harmony within myself when my life felt chaotic.

Years later I remember it in times when I feel lost or

overwhelmed with where life is taking me, I come back to this hour. Over the years, some of the words or questions answered have escaped my memory, but that feeling hasn't left me. The literal tattoo of this conversation remains as a gentle reminder to find the balance.

That day a seed was planted that began to grow, a feeling deep inside me, that I could only describe as a burning need to clear my karma...to find the balance and to become happier.

At this time in my life, if asked, I would've answered that I was very happy. I didn't understand that the happiness I felt was only happiness that was externally based. If things were going well, I was happy. If things were going my way, I was happy. If life was following my plan, I was happy. This is how many of us are, I'm no different...when things are easier, smoother, your way, or in your control, you're far more likely to be happy and content than when shit is hitting the fan. Those are the moments when happiness is hard to hold onto.

These moments of struggle and deep pain, are moments that I still struggle to find balance, to choose happiness when life isn't going my way is a hard thing to put into practice. We have been programmed that struggle and emotional turmoil are the norms, giving us few moments of happiness in between and us constantly seeking external factors to be able to feel happiness as often as we can. While afraid of and pushing down our more uncomfortable emotions that we don't deem "good" and have labeled as "bad".

That uncomfortable feeling of anger and rage as it vibrates through your body, your heart racing, nausea building, palms sweating and shaking...sweat building and rolling down various areas of your body. Feeling that level of rage towards someone or worse, towards yourself is a painful and scary feeling. One you wish would go away more quickly than it came on and one where the discomfort can grow so unbearable, that you ultimately reach a point of willingness to do anything for it to go away.

These darker times are so painful...the empty, tight feeling in your chest as you sit on the floor sobbing, unable to control the energy pulsing through you; followed by the release of emotions flowing at a rapid speed through your body as your grief begs to be seen.

These levels of intense emotions are ones that I'm deeply familiar with, and if you're reading this book, then you're also very intimate with these emotions. Or perhaps you've been shoving them down or ignoring them, and it's your desire to get more comfortable with your emotions in order to find that happiness that's waiting to burst out.

A piece that I want to share with you within this book is that it's totally OKAY to have and experience these emotions. Not only is it okay, but it's encouraged, welcomed, and celebrated; as these emotions are a part of you, and a part of your experience. Emotions are the energy within your body that's begging you to pay attention, to listen to yourself, and to begin to honor who is within you. No matter what, where, when, or how....these emotions will always play a role in your life, learning to embrace them is one path to your happiness...for to embrace your emotions, is to embrace and love yourself.

As I have worked over the past several years to clear my karmic patterns, learning to embrace my emotions has been a game changer. For so many of us, we are raised to ignore, push down, and contain our emotions; this does not benefit our bodies. It doesn't help the emotional or spiritual practice in any way. When we ignore our needs and emotions, we are only causing the energetic vibration of the body to reduce and this will ultimately manifest as disease, physical pain, depression, uncontrollable crying, apathy, and overall unhappiness.

Does any of this sound familiar to you?

I have moved through these types of emotions many times throughout my life, more so as I began my deeper spiritual practice, and became intentional of clearing karma within myself.

I first made the decision to clear this karma for myself in 2015 as I was moving through my divorce. I knew people who were older than me who were divorced, some had done a little work surrounding this experience, while others did no work at all. The ones who did no work on healing themselves whatsoever were bitter, unhappy, abusive, and overall miserable people. It was painful to be around them...I knew people who weren't even divorced but through one traumatic experience within their marriage harbored so much un-forgiveness, you could hardly be around them in any capacity.

These were people in my life who when they called, I would either avoid their phone calls as long as possible or take a deep breath each time I'd answer the phone...talk as long as I could hold space for their bitterness then develop some static or disconnection on my phone. I think we can probably each recognize at least one person within our life like this... when we look at them and ask, "What the hell happened to you?"

Perhaps we know their trauma story, or perhaps not...in any case their story isn't any of our business. The energy with which these individuals hold, the un-forgiveness and anger eats at them like a cancer and perhaps these individuals do develop cancer at some point in their life. They're often people that you may even have known before their trauma made them who they currently present themselves as today and you can remember a different version of them. Sometimes this makes it easier to keep these individuals in your life, sometimes it doesn't.

In the theory of Karma, we are each on our own journey. We each have lessons to learn, a path to walk, trials and tribulations to move through, and a life to experience. It, therefore, is not our place to dictate how one person should or shouldn't live their life, we can only have control of our own journey.

On our karmic path, we each make agreements, promises, oaths, etc with ourselves and other souls on this planet to come here to learn specific lessons, overcome certain tribulations and rise above to cultivate our deepest desires, of happiness and self-love. By the time we arrive in each lifetime, we forget these agreements, but the Universe still aligns it for us to learn these lessons, and overcome the hardships, giving us the option to choose happiness and love. Everyone we come in contact with on a close level plays a role in helping us to clear these lessons and return to the path of unconditional love.

Many religions on earth believe in the cycle of death and rebirth; according to Buddhist and Hindu beliefs, this is called Samsara...or reincarnation. This is where the spirit or soul cycles through each lifetime in various forms of all living creatures, based on the karma cleared and the journey taken within each life cycle.

I was raised in a Christian environment, where the idea of reincarnation didn't and doesn't exist, but the rebirth cycle does, it exists within this lifetime. In the spiritual community, this death and rebirth cycle is called, the Dark Night of the Soul...where your spirit goes through a transformation so deep and so profound that when you come out on the other side, you are reborn into a new person...still the same individual you but vastly different from before this experience. Some people even look or sound different, walk in a new way, and most definitely operate within their lives differently than they did before the dark night. A sense of calm or peace has settled over the body and their spirit has awakened to a deeper inner knowing of oneself with the ability to love and trust without falling prey to the narrative that the world provides.

In this space of the dark night of the soul is where you begin to clear your karma...whatever that may be. Where you begin to deeply learn your lessons, release unhealthy attachments, and clear energetic oaths, promises, and contracts within all your lifetimes.

Whether you believe in past lives, many lives, multiple dimensions, or just one life and that's it; each one of these lives builds up karma... Not only is karma built up in your lifetime, but in the lifetimes of your ancestors...your parents, grandparents, aunts, uncles, etc., and this is also passed on to you. Patterns of karma are taught, developed, learned, and carried on through lineages. So you don't have to believe in multiple lives to clear your karma, you can clear the karma of your ancestors both living and passed on for an equally powerful impact.

When you begin to work to clear karma you begin to see how much shit you're walking around with in your life. How many stories that you believe, are flat-out lies? How much shame, pain, anger, and unforgiveness has been passed on to you through the unhealed experiences of those who came before you? Or the lifetimes that you have lived previous to this one...perhaps even the lifetimes you are living in other dimensions, while you're currently living out this life. You begin to see how much fear, anxiety, and programming you have based on the experiences of those around you that have shaped how you view yourself and have become your way of being.

These are all karmic patterns that build up within yourself, your body, and your subconscious.

It can be really heavy shit to wrap your mind around, I can tell you that attempting to put logic to this will make your head spin and confuse the hell out of you.

So for the time being, as you move through this book, I ask you to be open to learning, exploring, and observing the karma that you feel you need to clear out. Each of us is different, you will go as deep as you desire to go...and if the Universe wants to take you deeper, then it will. Logic, will have nothing to do with it...allow yourself to be led by your spirit and by your intuition.

Since living in Bali, I have learned to be led by intuition and acts of karma more deeply than before coming here, as I witnessed how the Balinese inhabit this island through their spiritual practices. I am playing witness through the outside lens, of what a community looks like or can look like when they live on the basis of karmic belief. Like many other

cultures, there are many beliefs and thought processes practiced here among the Balinese Hindus; but what's attracted
me to this island is karma.

The Hindu beliefs on this island, are that of multiple lives,
that souls know one another from one life to the next, that
these souls reincarnate into other creatures depending on the
lessons they need to learn or the karma that they need to clear.
These incarnations aren't limited to that of human beings,
but all beings.

Karma is highly valued on this island. While people are
living within this lifetime, they have beliefs of clearing karma
through acts of kindness. One of these beautiful acts is that
the Balinese treat and call everyone "Friends." They will sit
down and talk to anyone, ask questions, be curious, make
statements...smile. At first, when you're not used to this behavior, you're asking yourself, "Why is this person talking to
me?" Then over time, you come to understand this is part
of the culture. The Balinese see that all living beings are connected and many are friends until proven otherwise. When
you are kind to someone else, you are bringing good karma
onto you and your family.

Through the belief that we are all connected as one, there
is also the defense or support of the community. When you're
good or kind to one person, they have the opportunity to
pass it along to the next person, or "pay it forward" as we say
in the West. This helps the community to grow and connect

together, helping the individual and family to receive good karma. Many Westerners living on the island adopt this way of being and this helps to feel less lonely when living far away...I can sit down anywhere and start talking to anyone, and 9 times out of 10, they are open to the conversation.

This belief in karma leads all the way through life and into the next life. When there is a death among the Balinese, the whole community celebrates the life of the individual who lived. It's referred to as a "Celebration of Life" because it's believed that they will see the soul of this person again in the next life, so there isn't a great sense of loss as we have in the Western world. There is an inner knowing that the soul will reincarnate and they pray that through the individual and community acts of good karma, they will move into a better life after death.

I have a Balinese friend with two children and she loves to tell me stories of her babies. She says, "They were for sure married in their last life, they fight like an old married couple. And he protects her like a father would, so he was also her father in a past life. They have had many lifetimes together."

I adore these stories as I love hearing about how these two children interact and also hearing it through the viewpoint of their mother. While she sees herself as their mother, because she is, she also sees herself as their guide and mentor, not their keeper or controller. They are not "hers", she views that their souls choose her to be their guide in this lifetime and she takes that role very seriously and with honor. She watches and observes the karma that they may have to clear out for themselves and that they came to help one another clear karma and create more good karma. She teaches them how to clear their karma the older they get, without controlling the situation, she lets them make their own choices.

We could sit here for days learning about the beliefs of these two cultures and how they compare to that of the Western world. For now, I am sharing this to broaden your perspective. When we're taught one way, as I was raised Christian, we forget that there are other ways of viewing the world. Other ways with which can greatly help us to navigate the uncharted territory of the healing and awakening journey. The exact journey that whether you realize it or not, we are moving through right now as a collective. On the rise are people talking about narcissistic behavior, seeking out healing modalities for trauma, understanding more deeply the impact our childhoods play out within our adult lives, and having the desire to clear out the shit in order to be happier.

WHY CLEAR OUT KARMA

When you make a decision to heal your life and clear karmic patterns, you're making dramatic life changes for yourself. These changes may not feel big at first but with consistency and dedication, little by little over time you will notice a change.

Clearing out karma is similar to when you begin to reduce the amount of caffeine you're having.

At first, you might not notice much of a change, as you keep consuming the caffeine off and on, but the more consistent you become and more dedicated to reducing your intake the more you notice changes. You might begin noticing you're really tired, or have headaches, you may need a nap when you haven't napped in years. It seems really hard during this stage to have such big changes to your body, but little by little with the commitment of reducing caffeine, when you completely get off the caffeine, your body no longer needs it. You notice you're sleeping way better at night, you have less brain fog, you feel happier, your headaches have gone and you don't need as many naps, and your hormones are more balanced. You were able to reach this more comfortable stage because you persisted and stayed consistent with the commitment you gave yourself to getting off or reducing caffeine.

So much happens in your life with the power of one commitment to make a positive change.

When you begin to clear out karma, you don't notice the change immediately...then one day it hits. The grief comes, you might get sick a few times, you're tired or irritable...you want to give up...but you don't. Then little by little you're not getting sick as often, you don't feel the waves of grief washing over you, you're not even irritable anymore...in fact, you're feeling pretty fucking happy! You have a sense of peace and relief and are totally proud of yourself for seeing it through and letting yourself ride the wave because now you feel fan-fucking-tasitc and want to share it with everyone!

Many people don't fully clear their karma to get out of the loop because when it gets hard, they give up. They slip back into old patterns, taking caffeine, or substance abuse, never being single or alone, working long hours, etc. When the emotions become too much they do anything and every-thing to distract themselves, making themselves feel better for a short while but it's just that, a short while.

Then before you know it they're back to the same old. Either back with the Ex who's toxic, not quitting the job that makes them miserable, eating like shit and the diet again didn't work, you name it, we slip right back into it when the times get tough. We've all done this from time to time or perhaps this is your pattern, it's human to revert back to the comfort zone when you've pushed your edges. This is part of the programming, we live from our logical head space, and the head is designed to keep us safe and out of danger, when you push your edges it feels scary and the head is like, "Hell no man, that's dangerous, let's go back and stay with what we know."

I say fuck that! That's a miserable experience no matter how you look at it, to consistently repeat patterns and to stay in the comfort zone that over time causes you to feel more and more miserable.

I visualize karma as a hamster wheel, which is what the loop is until you learn the lesson and make the decision to stop repeating it, you just go around and around...with little nuggets of pain stored in your body, the same way a hamster will store tiny bits of food in its cheek for a later snack, then jump in the wheel and run for a long ass time, going nowhere. This is how we repeat our own personal patterns and how patterns stay within families because as of yet no one has gotten off the hamster wheel.

It's so frustrating to WANT to do better but then be in such fear of yourself or of the unknown, that you stay on the wheel, not clearing your karma, not creating the life that's fulfilling, and letting the Universe take control, who will ultimately make you miserable until you're ready to make the change within yourself.

At this point, almost all of us make the decision to change. When we've become so unbelievably miserable the change is inevitable because we're willing to do anything to "make it better" or to "get off the wheel." We subconsciously have what we call a "Mid-life crisis", when you've been living in a pattern of some kind for so long, pretending you're okay when you're really not, then one day you've had enough and blow up your whole life.

This is when the karmic loop that you've been on becomes very, very obvious. So in your face obvious that you sit back to ask yourself how you didn't see it before. You see things when you're ready to see them and when you're willing to put in the work for the shift. Don't be too hard on yourself during this time, to see it is to be aware of it and this is exactly what you want, to be aware of the pattern so it doesn't keep repeating.

As you work to clear karmic patterns and to remove yourself from a pattern that's been playing out within this lifetime for yourself and/or your lineage; you will change those around you and assist in raising the vibration of the collective.

What does this mean, to assist in raising the vibration of the collective?

Everything has a vibration to it, emotions, words, actions, food, nature, everything. The vibration can be low or it can be high.

Currently and in the past, the collective is living in a low vibration. I write this coming off three years of a 'pandemic' where millions of people were living in fear, anxiety, depression, and other lower vibrating emotions. Through these three years and in the next few years to follow the collective is "waking up," seeing things that have been there the whole time, but are only ready to see the programming now. We're together, healing, making powerful changes, and this is raising the vibration of the earth.

Each corner of the earth vibrates differently but it's all one in the end. And the vibration can only rise when individuals are doing work on themselves to heal at their core and to find that happiness and love.

As you heal from your trauma so much in your life shifts, as you're probably already aware of. I often have come back to the quote, "It gets worse before it gets better"; this can be so true sometimes. If you go back to the message from the Monk, we need balance in our life. We need the rain for without it we wouldn't have the rainbow.

With this deep work, you also begin to heal your body and change your DNA. Scientists used to say that we have junk genes, this was the belief that most of our DNA had "no known purpose". Can you imagine that scientists tell us our DNA has "no purpose"? It's inherent in our DNA as a collective to find a purpose, live out that purpose, and be happy. If we're being told by authority figures we "have no purpose" for generations...then we wonder why there's so much misery in our society today. Without needing to read any more scientific evidence of someone else opinion, I disagree that we have "junk genes" that serve no purpose, I believe these pieces of our DNA have been forgotten by us and are no longer activated, therefore appearing to have no purpose. I believe these pieces of our DNA that are lying dormant have an insurmountable purpose to our ability as people to love more deeply, be happy, and live more harmoniously together.

We have been living disconnected and outside of ourselves

for so long that our DNA was physically reflecting this; your DNA had been programmed to think and act outside of yourself, rather than trusting yourself. As you heal spiritually and emotionally the physical body becomes stronger, yet less likely to put up with any bullshit...your health improves, your mind becomes clearer, your anxiety reduces, your stress reduces, your faith builds, and your trust in yourself grows stronger. The junk genes and programming that you or your lineage has been living in begin to heal and the unhealthy karmic patterns begin to dissipate. DNA clears diseases that's been running in families, harmful thought processes, etc. I believe in the coming years we will see more and more studies of DNA totally changing, people becoming more intuitive, more able to heal themselves with stronger immune systems, and other abilities we cannot even fathom.

This all comes with time, but it is there, available to you the more you heal yourself.

KARMA PLAYING A ROLE IN EMOTIONAL ABUSE

What you do affects those around you because of the vibration you are operating within and the vibrational broadcast you're projecting both consciously and subconsciously.

This goes back to taking responsibility for yourself, the more you do this the more others around you see it. We as a society are taught to blame one another or our environment for our shitty circumstances, to play the victim rather than take responsibility for ourselves, our actions, words, and life. While yes, external factors can sometimes play a role in many traumas, in today's age we have greater opportunities than ever before to take responsibility for ourselves, learn from the past, and heal.

In the day of my parents, who are Baby Boomers, going to therapy was for "crazy people." It was a shameful thing that NO ONE talked about, no one encouraged, and no one did unless something really fucked up happened. Today though, therapy is more widely accepted and encouraged than ever before. We're all out there doing our best and many people going to therapy to heal from those who still won't go to therapy.

As you heal yourself, through any modality, whether it be talk therapy, reading self-help books, working with a life coach, a TCM (Traditional Chinese Medicine) or an Ayurveda nutritionist, eating better, exercising, journaling, changing jobs, getting a divorce, etc. Whatever it is you're choosing to do to help yourself, you are also helping others.

How? You're leading by example. Those around you see it, whether they say anything or not, they notice...they see it because your vibrational energy has changed, something is different about you.

Your actions or words sometimes trigger them and they

react in a way that's comfortable for them or from a level that they're willing to go. Some will become inspired and want what you have...this can lead to them doing their own work. It can also lead to jealousy or envy if they aren't doing their work, they could become manipulative. This is when the work that you're doing comes deeper into play, you are developing the discernment to tell the difference between the two...the one who's out there being a Doer or the one who's out there playing a role. Both exist in your field now.

The more work you do the more opportunity you have to heal relationships around you. Be it those friendships that need mending or boundaries, or relationships with family that are often strained through unspoken words, you can have healthier relationship opportunities when you begin dating. So much is possible as you heal yourself, so many things that are on your level will come into your life.

Your past lives, future lives, and lineage will feel the effect of these changes. Sometimes the loop we are stuck on has happened in a past or parallel life, but when we close it and clear the karma in this life, it will affect our future soul's life and that of our lineage.

Many patterns are passed down through generations, which is why we have the saying, "It runs in the family." Sometimes the lifestyle patterns we get into are learned behaviors through our caregivers and those around us within our family. Narcissism and abuse are learned in childhood, when this is played out in adulthood we repeat the learned behavior often from a caregiver. So when you decide to leave emotionally abusive patterns, it affects the family, those living, those who have yet to come into this world, and those who have already passed on.

When you leave the cycle of abuse it helps those who are coming behind you, whether those are directly your children or not. It helps those to no longer have this pattern loop so deeply within their DNA. This allows them the opportunity to perhaps see these behaviors more clearly, as it will be taught to them differently. They will have a greater sense of self-worth, they will have firmer boundaries and they will be able to spot this behavior to make the choice for themselves if they wish to keep this person around or not.

It can take up to seven generations to clear a pattern out of a lineage. So those of us who do the deeper work, are able to quantum leap this process by removing the pattern altogether. In my personal experience, my mother began this process. She left abusive patterns within her family and did the work she knew at the time in order to teach her daughters differently. My mother married my father who is a kind and gentle man, vastly different to the men my mother had become accustomed to in her early life.

She taught us differently, but I still ended up in a narcissistic relationship, because she was the one to make the first move, I was the 2nd generation to leave this pattern. When my niece was born, I made the decision to do very deep work to quantum leap this process as much as possible. The idea of my beautiful, unicorn, and cosmic-loving niece ever being mistreated was a HELL NO for me. So while living in Bali in 2019, I looked in the mirror and said to Mama Bali, to the Universe, and to myself, "This ends with me." And my deep work began.

It's also so powerful as to be able to shift the energy of those who have passed on as well, including ones who were perhaps abusive or suffered at the hands of abuse. How? You may ask. Because you are still connected to them via the spirit world, those who have passed on and were more healed in their spirit can become guides for you in the living world. Those who were unhealed have an opportunity to shift their spirit through the action of your work. Some believe this gives them a better path to walk in the next lifetime.

Never underestimate the power that your healing journey will have on those around you, past, future, and present.

Making the decision to learn more about and clear your own personal karma has profound effects on your life, it will be a hard road at times. However, it'll be the most rewarding thing you'll ever do.

***

MANTRA

Here is a mantra that you're welcome to use or alter for yourself. Carry it with you as you read this book and embark on your healing journey. Begin to believe that you have the capability to make powerful and harmonious changes for yourself through this journey. I know full well that you do!

Mantras work in a way to reprogram the subconscious, if you repeat it verbally, using the vibration of your voice, write it down and think it over and over again, then it will become your new belief. Personally, I like to speak mantras out loud so that the body can hear and feel the vibration of your voice, this helps to reprogram the subconscious and the dormant lying DNA, into the new way of being.

Affirmation:
I am brave and strong by healing from my trauma.
I believe I have what it takes to see this through.
I am creating a happier life for myself.
I am worthy of loving myself more deeply.

2

Becoming Aware of Your Pattern

As you are working through the process of becoming aware of your karmic patterns playing out within your life, it's important to get curious about yourself. You hear often, "date yourself", and in a sense that's what you're doing, getting to know yourself, on a karmic level. Developing a deeper relationship with yourself, in order to love all parts of you as you are healing and walking away from these emotionally abusive patterns.

When you choose to do this work, it isn't always necessary to attach a story to what you're observing. This can sometimes and often get you stuck in the story or the emotions that is brings up...We start to believe the story that's playing out rather than saying, "This isn't me, this is a story." I had a friend who would frequently wear a T-shirt that read, "Believe none of what you think." It's so true! Our minds are designed to keep us safe so these stories that play out are the minds' way of keeping you in the comfort zone, rather than giving you space to leave the patterns behind.

In the physical the stories or believed programming, that are stored in the body are coming from somewhere, this is due to several factors:

First, physically: The stories are stored in the fascia, which is the tissues that encase muscles and blood vessels. Hence the saying, "Your Issues are in your tissues," we say this a lot as yoga instructors or somatic therapists. When you begin doing movements like yoga, somatic therapy, hiking, swimming, Tai Chi, or QiGong, you begin to release the stories within the fascia because you're moving the energy that's been stuck in those areas. At retreats, people will become an emotional wreck as the stories are coming up and being brought to their attention.

Exercise releases endorphins, which are your brain's "feel-good" neurotransmitters. Giving you more emotions such as, confidence, encouragement, happiness, ease and stress-free, sleep better, have less pain...all this from getting the body moving, because it releases the stagnation of the tissues, and allows you to let go of the stories. You become more capable of using the power of your mind to combat trauma or painful emotions.

The stories are also stored in the organs, in the form of

toxins, (environmental, chemical, Big Pharma, conventional cigarettes, alcohol, sugar, processed foods, etc.), blocked meridians, parasites, or deficient functioning organs. This is where not getting those emotions out of the body begins to cause physical or mental disease. There's a reason why eating right for your body, and getting movement is vital to your health, for all people. Society has sold us on the story, that "exercise is for when you're overweight" or to "avoid weight gain," however, the truth is that everyone benefits from some type of daily movement.

Second, emotionally: The stories are stored in your emotional body, and you can become addicted to feeling like shit because you've been believing some story about yourself that's keeping you blocked. Many of us, myself included, aren't always aware we do this until we take a step back to become observant. When we step back to see the bigger picture or walk away from a scenario, we see that it wasn't or is no longer serving us.

When the body is storing emotions, you may not be in touch with the emotional side so it manifests physically, in ways of not crying or crying all the time, constipation or diarrhea, along with most physical ailments acute or chronic.

I personally was completely unaware of this. I once lived life with daily migraines and diarrhea. Which had become a part of my life, it happened like clockwork for most of my life, over 30 years. It was all related to the fact that I was exposed to various abusive environments as I grew up, from daycare workers to manipulative teachers, to the members of the church my family attended or even family members themselves. All played a role in my physical health growing up. Healing from this has caused me to develop Chronic Fatigue, that's forced me to pay attention to my body, what I consume in any way, who I'm around, and what I'm doing to nourish or deplete myself. The fatigue is from my nervous system finally getting the rest and peace it deserves but in order to not give in to the story of, "I'll always be so tired," I need to really check in with myself regularly and listen to my body as I heal it.

During cognitive therapy, I had one of my earliest memories, which was being physically and verbally abused by my daycare facility, which was looking after a group of children. I observed and remembered this scenario as if it had happened to another child. It was still emotional as I witnessed adults being cruel to children, yet I didn't have a physical attachment to it. I confirmed the story with my parents, who had more of a reaction than I did. They had hoped it was a memory I would forget, seeing as I was only three years old at the time, but I have many memories, even younger, since doing work on myself to observe these moments that have caused deep trauma within my body.

I'm thankful in regards to this story and many others, as I was always honest with my mom, she said she realized when I was a toddler that I was someone who just spoke the truth and spoke up for what was right; so she always took time to listen to me. I told her what was happening at the daycare center, and she asked my dad to stake the place out. Within a few days, he witnessed my story and removed my sister and me immediately, calling the police.

I remember this too, sitting in a room and my dad bursting in yelling at these women, scaring the children half to death I'm sure. The women in charge shitting their pants as he burst in. My dad is a tall man, resembling a large mountain man, 6'3", long hair and beard, loud, booming voice...sweet as pie, scary as hell when he's defending his family. I remember the police arriving, my mom in tears and us sitting in the car until late as my parents helped the situation to keep the other children safe. The women in charge were horrible, I'm grateful that this lasted less than a few weeks. While it was brief, I consider this a karmic clearing in my journey.

When I look back on this memory, I see the core of who I am underneath the fear and self-sabotaging behavior, of an activist. A strong spirit who's not afraid to speak the truth, who says it without sugarcoating and often triggers people in the process, one who doesn't live in fear of authority but stands up to it. These are the types of viewpoints we can walk away from, seeing our light in the dark when we take time to become aware of the story, rather than focus solely on the pain experienced.

To give you a quick synopsis of the situation, the women

in charge at the daycare facility only wanted the children to watch TV. We were not allowed other activities, only watching TV. I didn't like to watch TV, I wanted to read books or play quietly to myself, they didn't like this and would physically assault me, and other children if we disobeyed or moved from the TV area. Additionally, they'd lock the babies, one of whom was my sister, into another room and let them cry all day. This made my little three-year-old, activist self, angry. I'd sneak into the baby room often to try to comfort them, upon which I'd get into major trouble. I remember being drug down a hallway by my hair and locked in a dark room because I was attempting to soothe my sister who'd been crying for longer than I thought she should have been.

I don't know how long I was in this room or closet, I eventually stopped crying and watched the shadows cross over the light coming through the bottom of the door. I remember sitting quietly, listening, and waiting for a chance to leave when it felt safe. The door was locked though, so I believe I eventually fell asleep. This moment put a fear of confined spaces and fear of the dark in me for most of my life, not knowing where it came from. Once I remembered this story, I was able to overcome both of these fears.

While I didn't remember this scenario for most of my life, it did affect me emotionally and physically, soon following this experience, is when I began getting migraines at the age of 5. I'd had digestive issues since I was born and gradually those worsened over the years, well into adulthood. Through my adult years when someone would yell, I could feel my body and spirit recoil in fear of being attacked. It wasn't until I identified where this came from that I was able to heal it and clear it. I still don't like when people yell, but I manage it with confidence rather than fear.

Third, in the DNA, which is why we say, "It runs in the family." This is a phrase we haphazardly use so often we don't realize what it actually means, all things run in the family until someone takes the time and dedication to address it. This can be a range of anything from disease to addiction, to emotional responses, to behavioral patterns...It'll all run in the family until it runs into the one who wants to clear it out.

You can begin to seriously address this when you begin to take a major shift in your health, looking at it from a holistic approach. Overhauling some of your current patterns for a new and healthier lifestyle that's more conducive to your personal needs. This alone is such a major change to the body, it eliminates parasites, raises the energetic vibration that you operate in, lifts the energy of the organ function, heals chronic or dormant disease, so, so much. Each person responds differently but in my experience, I've seen the biggest shift in myself and others around me by just shifting the lifestyle of what you're consuming from drinks, food, TV / Movies, shopping, etc.

Your DNA is a storage unit of data, just like your computer hard drive, storing data in the form of a series of 0's and

1's...we are a walking USB / Hard Drive. When you begin to understand the power that your DNA holds you're able to completely reprogram yourself, the patterns, and the stories. This is why we say your multiple lifetimes are stored in your DNA, the stories or disease that your parents and ancestors hold is in your DNA, and the Universe is in your DNA.

As mentioned in the previous chapter, we have inside the body what's being called, "Unplugged" or "Junk" DNA, which is pieces of who we were as a collective and who our ancestors were that have been separated due to the trauma or stories that are being held in the body. This is how we have become disconnected from our bodies to not be able to identify emotions, listen when we need rest, understand disease, follow intuition, be connected to nature, and so much more.

You can really take a deep dive into the DNA and its power, I highly suggest that you do, it's truly fascinating and will blow your mind at the power that your body actually holds. Scientists are recently discovering that memories can be passed down through DNA, for up to Fourteen generations, hundreds of years, thousands of people before you.

Another fascinating (recent discovery to science) but well-known among indigenous worldwide is the power of water. Our bodies are comprised of 70% - 80% water, water holds memory. When you speak to water, you have the ability to change its memory, its composition, and its effectiveness on the body. So when you're speaking to your body, the water molecules can shift, change, and enhance or they can decrease in effectiveness.

Lastly, there's spirituality: The stories we tell ourselves are also stored in the spiritual realm, through past lives, lineage, parallel universes, oaths, contracts, curses, hexes, agreements, etc. When you believe that you've lived many lives, then you'll come to understand that a lot of what we carry can come from these spiritual spaces. This is the part that's hard for many to understand, and it's all so open to interpretation. It's only able to be explained once you've lived it and experienced something so otherworldly, that you say to yourself, "Hmmm" That's all that comes out sometimes, just a sound.

When you combine all of this together, the physical, emotional, spiritual, and DNA, it's not hard to see why we as a collective and individually remain on this hamster wheel. When I was put into the closet, unbeknownst to me, my great-grandmother had also been locked in a room and unable to leave. The DNA memory activated within me, instilling a fear that had been placed there before I arrived on the planet. I could've chosen to remain in that fear of being locked in somewhere or I could choose to work it out and move through it.

This is why I asked at the beginning of the book to have an open mind and not try to wrap too much logic around the spiritual aspect, once you begin experiencing it, as I'm sure you already have from time to time, it becomes tales that when you recount to friends you follow it with, "I swear, because I cannot make this shit up!" Some believe you and some look at you a little funny, both are appropriate responses. You can't make it up, it's either woo-woo or your imagination but either way, it's real for your journey.

This is a lot to consider but as you practice observing more and more, it will all become second nature then over time you'll process these things in a matter of minutes as you're washing a sink full of dishes. When you're finished, you're feeling grounded, confident, and clear about the topic you were observing within you. Self-observation is a developed emotional muscle, like going to the gym to build physical muscle, it takes time, so be patient and have some grace for yourself.

You're making a lifestyle choice by choosing to clear karmic patterns of emotional or otherwise abusive behaviors. This is something that you'll do over and over again as you age, each time will become easier, more smooth, less resistant, more supported, and more compassionate, as you stick with it. Which I highly encourage you to do.

So how do you do this? Observe. Play back a scene for yourself and watch objectively, without judgment or criticism, almost as though you're watching a movie. When you're watching a movie, you're invested in playing witness to the storyline unfolding, getting to know the characters, curious about the plot, and if you can predict the ending. Sometimes we become so invested that emotions are brought forth, and this is okay, it's normal and encouraged. Watch this scene of your patterns, to learn and educate yourself, be invested to a level where you can be invested, like a movie, but not to be attached to the story.

When you're not attached to the story, it becomes like watching a movie, you have the emotions, and you can identify with a character but you end the movie knowing that it's not who you are. You're not that character, it's just a piece of you and you don't need to be attached to its storyline.

For example: A piece of who I am and was, is a woman who was in a series of emotionally abusive relationships. That doesn't make me a victim, it doesn't make me have pity for myself and it doesn't mean it will continue to happen on repeat. It was a past part of myself, pieces of all the elements that came before me that I played out. However, I myself am not easily emotionally abused nor am I emotionally abusive to others. The pattern played out and ended with me.

OBSERVING THE KARMIC LOOP WITHIN MYSELF

I'd like to give you a small glimpse into my life and thought processes before I came to marry someone with narcissistic behavior. I believe there were many moments in my life that led up to me being in this type of relationship, I wasn't aware of them at the time, but through the years of my healing journey,

I can see that the stories implanted in childhood play a role in where we go or who we become in life. They especially play a role in how we show up in a relationship and who we end up choosing as a partner or why.

Throughout my childhood, I never felt good enough. I can remember myself crying inconsolably as young as ten, saying, "I'll just never be good enough." I have this vivid memory of my mom kneeling in front of me repeating over and over, "No Johnna, you are perfect the way you are." This was a story that I came to this earth with, I feel it's one that's been passed down to me through my lineage, and energetically broadcasted by an extended member of my family, who didn't believe that women were ever good enough. As a child, I didn't understand this story but it was already seeded so the roots slowly grew.

I am a very highly sensitive person, and as a child, I was very easily upset by negative or hostile emotions, though I often still am. My mom has told me she and my dad realized when I was a toddler that they couldn't argue or firmly speak to one another in front of me, as a result, I would just break down in tears. So for the most part they learned to argue behind closed doors and express their emotions in their own time. They adjusted and became softer humans when I came along because I was unable to manage any outside emotions. I can probably count on one hand the amount of times my parents have yelled at me, the way parents sometimes do. They quickly adopted a gentle parenting method with me, speaking to me calmly and rationally in order for me to learn.

In my teenage angst years, I was still unable to process emotions, only this time it was mine and I became the one to yell, and my parents often responded in a calm and collected manner. Sometimes I feel as though it was they who invented the term, "gentle parenting," as they knew they needed to change their behavior to be able to connect to me, gain my trust, and teach me valuable pieces of life.

Despite their best efforts, I still carried this story that was so deeply rooted, that it affected all corners of my life. Giving me huge amounts of insecurity, shyness, and timidity; I was easily angered and projected my emotions onto others because I had so many spilling over. I now know myself to be a highly intuitive person, and more so as a child...However, intuition wasn't the theme of society, so it wasn't strong in my circle of peers or outside of our home. My parents did teach us intuition as children, but I believe when we began getting into the church, intuition was no longer the focus and it was "God's will" instead. I battled this greatly, because "God's will" or the teachings of the Christian Bible went against my intuition most times, causing me to feel confused or angry as I aged into pre-teen and young adult. The teachings of the church deepened the story of "not enough" and unworthiness, roots that were unknowingly growing into deeply embedded stories as I grew into an adult.

There have been many times in my life when I have been diagnosed and suffered through depression, while only once where I took any prescribed anti-depressants. My first memory of a very dark depression was, the time in my life when I was prescribed Pharma and consumed the prescription at the most impressionable age. I was a teenager, around fifteen to seventeen years old; hormonal, trying to figure myself out as my life changed rapidly every day...I'd say if we base depression on hormonal changes, then every teenager in the world would need it from time to time and that's just not true. Hormones play a major role in how you feel and what you think. If your hormones are out of whack so is your thought process, your organ function, and your brain function...leading to just about everything a teenager is diagnosed with these days.

In addition to hormone imbalance are the health and vitality or lack thereof, of the nervous system. Depending on what you have going on in your life, at any given age the nervous system plays a huge role in how you will manage the situation. The nervous system will send the body and mind into fight, flight, or freeze mode. Causing one to either avoid it at all costs, run away from the pressure, or freeze and have a hard time progressing or growing in life. Your nervous system is partly a learned behavioral trait from childhood in watching those around you react to life. As you watch these reactions you register that this is the way to respond to life and as you grow up, you ultimately have the same responses...This is why we say things like, "I sound like my mother" or "Your father would do that too." It's because you inherit your nervous system from your parents through the DNA and also by watching the behavior.

During this time when I took the pills, I lost a whole year of my life. I don't remember most of my seventeenth year on this planet...I was on so many pills, my mind shifting, my hormones out of whack, daily migraines, IBS, Chrones, fainting spells, anxiety...All just to name a few. I didn't know how harmful these tiny compressed tablets would become, after all as my doctor prescribed them, telling me it was okay. I believe this time of my life and these pills to have shaped the next twenty years of my adult life, in how I viewed the world, the stories that I told myself. Ultimately becoming my way of being and relating to the world around me.

Unfortunately, in my teenage years, this wasn't the time I overcame depression...This all led me to take pills for over ten years to combat emotional turbulence and periodical self-harming well into my college years. I began to get a grip on it all in college though, seeing new people and hearing stories of other people and what they did or didn't do to self-medicate and cope with their life. I didn't feel so alone in my struggle, I then learned and unlearned new behaviors.

I recognized how deeply troubled my body was but because I was the only one around me suffering to this degree, I hid it and coped with it as best I could. I became a vegetarian before it was the thing to do because I was unable to digest meat, twenty-plus years later it still makes me sick. Living with this story of "not enough" deeply rooted in my subconscious, it was wreaking havoc on my body, developing into so many diseases and ailments. Over the years the doctors would tell me that these would be lifelong issues.

I began to stop listening to this story of being sick my whole life around the age of eighteen when I stopped eating meat after reading a book about a man suffering from Crones and the eating methods he took to live again. Taking my health into my own hands, without knowing what the hell I was doing was my first small step into valuing myself more. I was still eating a lot of processed foods though, which kept parasites in my body and therefore kept the story alive for many more years.

It took many years though to get myself the therapist that I needed to help me with my understanding of myself and accepting of loving myself. It was post-college that I asked my parents to help me pay for therapy...I had asked this before in that blurry teenage year, unfortunately, this time the answer was the same, "You don't need that, it will be okay." At this time my mom told me everything would be okay, and "This too shall pass".

While she was right, it did pass, at that moment of my life, I needed more. I needed help and guidance that I couldn't find in my prayers or in the Bible or talking to a trusted friend. I needed someone to guide me on how to help myself because I felt as though I was flailing... unsure where to go, what to do, or how to do it. It was that next round of formidable and vulnerable years where my life was upside down. I was in the working field full time for the first time, not near any friends, not in college life anymore, and single after recently being cheated on by my college boyfriend.

Cue this story of "not enough" to take an even deeper root in my body, inside my subconscious, and not let go until many years later. I didn't know this was happening at the time, so I had no way to navigate through it. I did the only thing I knew to do, cope and distract, I shifted my coping strategies, to drinking more alcohol and taking fewer pills. In my mind and in reality, it did help…For a while, it helped me to shove it down and distract myself from how I was really feeling. It gave me the "liquid courage" that I needed to be vulnerable and open up, to of course my drunk friends as we'd sit and cry into our beers. Having a crowd of people whom I could drink with and find support helped me to feel seen and accepted for the first time in my life.

This is how it is with our emotionally wounded patterns or self-harm, it can manifest in any form when we feel a deep sense of unworthiness or unlovable. I certainly felt unlovable. The story was one I didn't know was even playing out as a lie, one that I believed to my core. Since this was my belief and the vibration that I put out into the world, I unconsciously and through the Universe found myself in repeated situations that validated this story of unworthiness. Keeping me in the loop, in the karmic cycle of being treated like shit by those around me, after all, I felt so unlovable so it only made sense to me in my distorted viewpoint.

Ram Dass teaches that awareness is eternal and change is inevitable. I was eternally aware of my story but was so resistant to the inevitable change that I spent years coping with a story out of fear of change. We do this over and over and over. Resist change because we are afraid of it, so we live in resistance to change of and then re-live the same pattern over and over. I was so unwilling to sit with my story of unworthiness because I didn't want it to be there, so I hid it, I resisted it, I coped with it, I avoided it, yet I vibrated within it...Perpetuating my cycle of not loving myself and not feeling worthy of love from others.

When I AM loving awareness, I am able to love myself, "flawed parts" and all.

When YOU ARE loving awareness, you are able to more deeply love yourself, "flawed parts" and all.

Begin to be aware of the abusive karmic pattern that you need to clear within yourself as you read more of my story within this pattern.

BEING AWARE OF STAYING IN THE PATTERN OUT OF FEAR

I had my first job post-college that I didn't like but stayed because I was too afraid to move to another position, I was staying in my comfort zone. Because I felt as though I needed to find another job but wasn't, the Universe took care of this for me when I was abruptly laid off. The day before this I made an executive decision, that my boss didn't like, after yelling at me in front of the rest of the staff and throwing fabric swatches at me, she came in the next morning to tell me my job was being closed out. I knew this to be a lie and when I picked up my last check the following week another person was sitting at my desk. So I got first-hand experience of the unsteadiness of the workforce and what I picked up was the lesson, "Don't piss off your boss." This caused me to move into my next job still in fear of the last one.

I soon found another job, only weeks later. This employer turned out to be one whose personality and mood swings were one where I never knew who'd be showing up for work that day. One day they were sweet as pie and a true friend, compassionate, eager to teach, and excited for me to learn. The other days they'd be nothing short of abusive, with lots of curse words, yelling, throwing things...I was hit several times over the head for my unknowing mistakes and called stupid more times than I cared to count. These moments triggered that little girl who was hit at the daycare. Confused, sitting at my desk holding my head like, what in the actual fuck just happened....Here I was a woman in my mid-20s being abused by her female employer.

My coworker would do her best to defuse the situation

and one other flat-out yelled at the employer to have more respect...usually my co-workers told me to go home or take a break to get out of the field of the employer. I'd just sit there in shock, not saying a word, tears burning behind my eyes, nausea building in my stomach, unable to respond or stand up for myself. I'd usually just follow the direction of my co-workers and get out of the line of fire from my employer, I often was her scapegoat for frustration.

At this point in my life, I hadn't started any emotional or spiritual healing work, my health was always the main focus, so I was telling myself that it was all my fault...If only I'd known what I did wrong so that I didn't set her off. This thought process is the inner child being completely afraid of the adult, not knowing how to respond or what to do, and blaming themselves for the problem. Totally unaware that this was not appropriate behavior for an employer, I had been around screaming employers any time I was not working for my parents. At this point, I thought this was the way that it was, and I wasn't wrong in my assumption, that many, many employers are this way, completely unable to manage their emotions, and in my opinion, shouldn't be in leadership roles. Don't confuse these abusive-style people under the leadership role, they are not leaders! These are people who have no business stepping into the managerial role and claiming to lead others.

This is one thing that's wrong with our society as a whole: We view people in leadership roles as leaders when they are unhealed children, leading from their wounded space. Starting wars, fights, lies, manipulation, and controlling others out of fear…This is not leadership as we have been calling it, this is abuse of power and abuse of others.

So if you have a current or ex-partner who likes to hold the "leadership" role, yet acts this way, they are not a leader, they are in the weaker position. They're unhealed and deeply wounded individuals who hurt others to make themselves feel better. This is not a partner, this is not a spouse, this is not a friend, this is someone to distance yourself from as quickly as you can, and use the BLOCK button on your phone.

The outburst with my employer would happen every six to eight weeks or so, with myself, other employees, and personal family members, it was a very unstable and toxic work environment. Instead of leaving though, I worked there for a few years and just got used to it, learning to cope and manage the stress. This was a time during the recession when millions were out of work, so I lived in fear of no work and through this scarcity mindset, I just stayed.

Do you see that my pattern and choices here were that of an abuse victim, that of someone believing to the core they have no other option? Because of this belief, I stayed in an unhealthy workplace, living in fear and limited thinking. The truth for all of us is that we always have options, this allows you space to breathe rather than suffocating in the belief that there's nowhere else to go. When you think you don't have options, zoom out, look at the bigger, broader picture to see what's available to you, think outside of the box, and be willing to get out of your comfort zone. Opportunities will present themselves everywhere as soon as you say in truth that you're willing to leave your comfort zone for something better.

While I was at this job, in an unstable environment, afraid to tell anyone what was happening, is when I met my ex-husband. I was already living in this emotionally abusive cycle, partying a lot when I wasn't at work, and dating men who exhibited narcissistic behavior. I was totally unaware of what patterns to look for as I was eyeballs deep in it already.

It took me meeting my ex-husband and sharing stories with his father for his father to tell me, "That's bullshit Johnna, you don't deserve that...Don't go back to work." We were out to lunch eating Mexican food when his dad spent the whole hour encouraging me to not go back to work at all, "Don't even get your things. Leave them! Don't go back". He was telling me to leave an abusive situation and I didn't, because of my limited thinking and fear mindset. He spent the next year that I reminded at that job taking me to lunch once a month and encouraging me to just not go back. He'd say, "Do one of those, go to lunch and never go back...Delete their number and don't answer, make it mysterious and let them wonder whatever happened to you!" We'd laugh and I'd say, "I could NEVER do that, it's not an option." Not to mention the anxiety that would come up thinking of not following through with my word…The stories were deeply layered to keep me in these abusive cycles.

Due to my resistance to the change that I needed to make within myself, the Universe took over again for me. This was the time in the US when the economy was in the shitter and I was eventually laid off again, with almost a month's notice to find another job, complete with a letter of recommendation.

This was the exhibition of the compassionate part of my employer, she cried letting me go, telling me how great of an assistant I was, and thanking me for putting up with her bullshit. She even took the step to make calls to offices across the city to see if they were hiring, and to help me find another job. She found me a short-term, part-time job at another office close to my house, which helped a lot financially, and my ability to forgive her for the other shit.

Still, a tactic of an abusive personality is to buy things, over apologize or go out of their way in order for you to view them as a good person, trying their best. A way to absolve themselves of their sins. It's a manipulation tactic, one that's so unnoticed by those around this person, that it allows for when they have their outbursts, to quickly forgive them because they're doing something nice. Granted in small ways we all do this when we feel guilty for hurting another person, do something nice for them as a gesture of apology…the problem in this lies when this is a repeat pattern and not an every so often thing.

When I mentioned this is the problem with our society, people in leadership roles who are deeply wounded and create abusive environments in the name of compassion or the ever common, "because I/we care". This is not true compassion though, I'd like to encourage you to begin to shift your perspective to see this as a tactic of manipulation. We have become so used to this behavior in our society that we have never seen it for what it is...This is the classic phrase, "I control you because I love you." We are used to this as a collective because parents, religions, governments, companies, and partners, do this exact thing. So when it happens the body responds, the soul screams, the heart is broken, then the mind creates logic and excuses. We remain conflicted within ourselves, remain in fear, and then have a hard time walking away and staying out of the loop because everyone around us is telling us that we're wrong.

In a healthier environment when someone has an outburst, it will never get to the abusive level. An apology doesn't need gifts or something extra, it needs a change in behavior...if an apology is associated with no change in behavior, then it's not a true apology and it's a distraction from the abuse or manipulation.

Developing awareness and discernment to be able to identify between the two is very important in this type of environment. Some of the nicest people you know can be manipulative because this is a trained behavior for our society.

It doesn't always get to the abusive level so when it's manipulation, it can be spoken to and resolved more easily if that person, or yourself are willing to make the change within the self.

When I lost this job, I was so excited to be laid off! I was blissful to be out of the environment and made the decision that if that were to ever happen again, I'd be out and unemployed before staying another day. I would absolutely "Go to lunch and not return," leaving them to wonder about whatever happened to me.

I became aware that I had allowed myself to be wildly mistreated, manipulated, and abused, all while getting paid for it!! I allowed the behavior of my employer because I didn't have the courage to stand up for myself, to walk out of that office. I didn't know I had options. Losing my job allowed me to see that I did have options, we always have the option to make a different decision, to walk away, and to create a healthier environment.

When we live in fear, we will keep ourselves in really shitty situations or unhealthy environments for far too long. Telling ourselves the lie that there are no other options, but the truth is, we always have options. In my case, I lived between my boyfriend's house and my parents, so I had a place to live, I could've asked for financial help or at the very least put my resume out there to be seen while still working for this employer.

So why didn't I at least try? I didn't have faith in this scenario that I would be taken care of or that something new would come to me that would be even better if I'd left this situation. I was living so deeply in the story of, "I'm not going to make it on my own", that I didn't ask for help, nor share what was happening. I unknowingly locked myself inside my own prison. I didn't have the awareness or courage to really make the change, so the Universe did it for me by letting me be laid off. When we don't leave our toxic patterns, at some point the Universe will step in to give us the opportunity to make healthier choices to step out of the pattern.

When you're willing to leave the toxic environment and become more aware of the situation, the Universe will always provide for you. It's a matter of believing this to be true and getting into alignment with where you want to go, then the Universe lays it out.

After shifting my energy, I quickly found a job less than two weeks later...It was one where I wasn't abused and my employer enjoyed my company. She frequently gave me raises and praised my hard work...I worked there for a long time until it was time to move on. It was a job I needed...It certainly came with its lessons and frustrations but it allowed me to stop drinking and partying so often, I didn't feel the need to escape as often as I did in my previous employment.

It was one who for the most part my time was respected

and valued...which is more than I can say for the previous job. I was seen for my value of what I could bring to the company, as a person and a designer. It was in this job that I made more money and began to really shift my life. Still, though, I wasn't aware of the stories I was living in that would keep me repeating abusive patterns for a few more years.

***

JOURNAL PROMPTS:
On a scale of 1-5
(1 being Not Willing, 5 being I am Willing):

- Are you willing to look at the stories you hold?
- Are you willing to change in environments where you have stories holding you back?
- Are you willing to see the red flags you've been ignoring?

Sometimes we aren't willing to do anything about shifting a pattern, that's okay, perhaps that's where you are right now. By acknowledging the pattern of unworthiness this acknowledgment alone will begin to make shifts in your life, to where ultimately you will be in a space where you'll become willing to address it and clear it out.

- What pattern is playing out within your life?
- Examine all aspects of your life, work, home, friendships, family, and society - does anything pop up that is a pattern repeated within these areas?
- What beliefs of unworthiness are you holding?

Look at your childhood:

- How were you raised?

- What stories did your parents teach you or try to instill?
- What stories did others try to discourage within you?
- Do these 2 stories go together?

When examining past or present relationships, how do these promote or dismantle the story of unworthiness within you?

What does compassion mean to you?

How can you show yourself more compassion in these situations?

Where is your intuition asking you to pay the most attention? (First thing that comes to mind, go with it, don't doubt.)

3

Getting Out of the Comfort Zone

I didn't know I had been depressed in my previous job as I mentioned last chapter. I didn't realize that I was out of spiritual alignment within my relationship with myself because everyone in my circle was also living a similar or the same lifestyle. We lived in it together and perpetuated the cycle of being so emotionally overwhelmed with our lives, yet not knowing how to help ourselves or if we even wanted to. I'd been in it for so long and so were the adults around me, that this was life.

Many of my friends would tell me, "Johnna, you don't belong in this lifestyle, you're not meant for it and you're going to do better things."

The problem? I didn't want to do better things...I didn't

want to be alone, to stop drinking and partying, to stop the cycle I was in because I could feel in my gut that I would lose my lifestyle and friends, and I wasn't ready to give that up. I didn't want to be different, I wanted to fit in, only I was forcing myself to fit where I was quickly and unknowingly outgrowing. I didn't like the lifestyle but it was the first time in my life I felt like I belonged. My friends were amazing people, and always happy to see me. When we disagreed I wasn't their scapegoat, we were raw and honest with our feelings and one another. Sometimes it hurt like hell to hear my truth but I'd also tell them theirs...We were doing our best to be compassionate with one another.

We didn't know how to be compassionate to ourselves but we sure as shit could put it on for our friends and give outwardly, we are good at that in Texas. Slowly this shifted though, we would catch one another talking shit about ourselves, and reply with, "Would you say that shit to me? No! You would not, so why say it about yourself?" A new response was developed that after talking poorly about ourselves, one would need to recite 3 amazing things we love about ourselves, to counterbalance the negative.

I remember getting ready to go out with my best friend and talking shit about myself when she called me on it. She walked over to me, told me to look in the mirror, then to say three nice things about myself, we weren't going anywhere until I did. It took me a few minutes and redo my mascara after tearing up, but I did it. This was my first taste of self-love work. After doing this more often, even alone, I started to actually like myself, a lot!

Once I became engaged, was when I wanted to get my shit together. I used to get extreme and irrational road rage, then my fiancé told me, "You'll never drive with our kids if you keep acting like a lunatic behind the wheel." With this, I knew he was right and I needed to get a better grip on my emotional responses somehow...so I did the most popular thing that was on the rise...Yoga.

I'll never forget it...I bought a class pass at a studio near my home, yoga clothes, a mat, and a water bottle...I was ready to do Down-Dog or whatever it was called. I booked my first class, drove to the studio, parked, and watched the people filing in...I began to get so sick...my head started hurting, I felt lightheaded, my stomach started moving, fear washed over me and I froze...I stayed sitting there in my truck and missed the class. Driving home crying, screaming at myself, "WHAT IS YOUR PROBLEM!?! GET IN THERE, YOU NEED THIS! FUUUCCKKK!!!" And a whole bunch else that just isn't nice to repeat. All for what, because I was too nervous to walk into something totally foreign, out of my comfort zone, and taught through Christianity that Yoga was a connection to the Devil.

I can't at all see why I was so nervous to make this move....(I say with an eye roll).

We can sometimes be so hard on ourselves when compassion is needed most. This can go back to how our society is, concealing compassion behind abuse so we learn to be abusive to ourselves, calling it "tough love." I encourage you to take this small story and reflect it onto your life, find true compassion for yourself when moving out of your comfort zone, it can be both scary as hell and thrilling.

Getting outside of your comfort zone and re-programming your perspective is scary-ass shit! Not only was I trying something new but I was going against the grain of what I had been raised to believe, I was stepping out in secret mind you, to go do yoga. There was no way in hell I was going to tell anyone about this, I knew they'd talk me out of it and I didn't want that to happen. I wanted yoga, it was calling to me and had been for so many years, I was excited to try this but also scared of what it would do. I heard it improves your life, but how, why, what was its magic? Where was this form of movement going to take me?

The next week, I tried again. I booked my class, drove to the studio, watched the people file in, and watched some more, breathing deep breaths and telling myself, "If you don't like it just don't go again but at least you tried something new."

So I got out of the car and started walking, checked my name off the list, and stepped through the door. I looked around to see at least 70 people in the room, smiling, hugging, waving, and happy to see one another...Then doing the same thing to me! A total stranger! "What in the hell have I just signed up for??" Was my only thought at that moment. I grabbed a spot in the back by an older Asian woman who smiled so sweetly at me, and I followed the flow.

"HOLY SHIT WHERE HAS THIS BEEN ALL MY LIFE??" I was instantly hooked. By the end of the class, I was hugging the teacher, talking to the woman next to me, and asking her about the Mala beads she was wearing, "Where can I get a necklace like that?"

I drank the Kool-Aid. It was all uphill from there!

After this, I joined a book club with some women that I met online through a meetup app. I was taught never to meet people online, they would "obviously kill me". But since I went to yoga and found out it wasn't meeting the Devil, I thought, "Let's test this theory also." Dangerous in some circumstances I know, but this specific scenario felt good, I was following that intuition despite what others around me were saying.

About six months go by, and nothing has changed in my outward life but I sure as shit changed inwardly. I started declining brunch to go to yoga or work out. I was really enjoying the book club of moms, that I joined a 2nd book club, then left my first book club to start my own! I was on a roll...It was during this time that I changed so much that even my hair colour changed. I went from dark blonde to brown naturally...My DNA was changing and I had no clue!

Life was fucking great at this point. I had reduced my Pharma pill intake by half, was eating healthier, no gluten, going to yoga, smoking more weed and drinking less wine, reading more books, and watching less TV. I was at a job I liked with coworkers who were real friends. I had a friend circle of solid women who while we partied, were low-key...Not in the bars or clubs anymore, drinking at home in the pool and swapping food recipes. I was blissful.

I was also oblivious to the things around me that were major red flags. While my current life choices were better for me, they were still not getting to the root of my issues of WHY I felt unworthy and still kept me living in fear, though I was expanding out. I was right where I was supposed to be, making bigger and bolder steps, healthier choices, and doing what was making me happy. This was the first time in my life I was truly moving through these steps, in my late 20s, feeling really proud of myself.

THE AWAKENING PERIOD

Then things shifted in a major way when my home life called my attention. I had been with my boyfriend (soon to be my fiancé) for almost 5 years and I began having dreams of my future. I was feeling strongly that he and I should break up. To my current state of awareness, nothing was really wrong on the surface but this feeling that things needed to shift, that I was in the wrong place, living a life that suited others around me, but internally didn't suit my desires at all. I wanted to live abroad, travel, see the world, and live on an island, something I had only shared with him, to which his response was hard, "Not going to happen".

I felt that we were growing to be incompatible...at the time I had never heard of the term, "gaslighting" but was beginning to recognize that this was happening quite a lot. He'd say or do one thing, then deny it to me later and I would question my reality, ultimately agreeing that he was right and I was wrong. He'd do things for me, then when I asked for help somewhere, he'd take time to recount all that he'd already done as a support for him not fulfilling my request. It wasn't feeling good to me, I felt alone, unsupported, and really insecure about the stability of the relationship. I had worked through these emotions on my own, not telling anyone and coming to the conclusion that it was time to break up and go our separate ways.

I talked to my closest people about breaking up with him, but they talked me out of it, giving me so many reasons why that would be the "wrong decision." I listened to their opinions over my intuition, doubting my ability to choose for myself, so I stayed. When he proposed a few weeks later...I accepted. I accepted even though my intuition told me not to...I had almost never followed my intuition, and this time I did what I was good at, doubting myself to go with the logical solution. I did love him, we had fun together and we wanted the same things…or so I thought. We'd been together a long time and it was the next step, right?

It was a few months into the engagement that I started getting those familiar feelings of feeling alone and unsupported again. I was going through the motions of everything but things just didn't feel right. He kept telling me all the things I was doing wrong that caused my feelings of aloneness, plus his mom (a person who was narcissistic and very emotionally abusive) was heavily involved in our lives, also telling me things I was doing wrong. She would frequently argue with me when I would go against her word or attempt to stand up for myself. So I sunk deeper into self-doubt and unworthiness, over time believing that he knew best. For most of my young adult life I'd been told what to do so much by others that through my illnesses and exhaustion, I listened and started trusting people outside of myself more and more.

The stress of planning a wedding was slowly becoming too much for me, my health was declining, and I was overwhelmed, I didn't want a big wedding but he did, so bigger is what we did. I would frequently remind his mother that it wasn't her wedding and she didn't have any say in the things we chose. Several times I'd asked him if we could elope, do a small distance wedding, and just cut our losses with the deposits we'd put down. At this point, his mom was so obsessed with getting her way in our wedding, that it was taking any and all joy out of the process. I realize this is sadly a "normal" thing to happen when planning a wedding but for me, his inability to see her input as a problem was a red flag I was choosing to ignore.

Here I was getting married for what I believed to be the only, long-lasting time and I was letting everyone around me control the situation. I believe this is when my mom and other people started noticing his behavior because they'd all say, "If it's not what you want, don't do it." But I didn't believe this to be an option, so I went with the plan of the bigger wedding and did my best to argue my need for simplicity and minimalism.

The stress eventually began getting to him as well, only he had a different response, and he began becoming more controlling and demanding. At one point, he wanted me to end a friendship with a good friend because of her chosen lifestyle...I fell back into my story that had been stashed away, "I was again...the problem, I wasn't good enough" and I was so afraid of it all imploding, I couldn't bear that shame. He told me if I couldn't choose "the right friends", then how could he trust me with being his wife or with more responsibility? He was offended by my friend, and it then became my responsibility, something that I needed to repair for him in order for him to be happy.

This statement began getting used a lot, "If you do (this), I would be happy", so I began to go into overdrive. Society teaches us that we should "make others happy;" it doesn't teach us to take responsibility for ourselves but instead to blame others or expect them to make us feel a certain way. I began doing my best to make him happy, I'd tell him it was something he should do for himself, but he assured me it was the responsibility of a wife, and I needed to get used to it. Red flag much! I didn't see it though as a red flag. At the time I was very disconnected from myself and though I would be angry with this expectation, I didn't see my anger as a sign that something needed to change. I instead would say my anger was not willing to comply to make him happy and then I turned the anger onto myself for falling short.

Since I was back living out my story that "I couldn't do anything good enough", I knew at this point I needed extra help, "to make me better." I asked my fiancé, who made a decent amount of money to help me pay for therapy...the answer was one I'd heard before, "You don't need therapy, don't waste your money".

So I didn't waste my money but was determined to do it, I looked at my finances to see what I could afford. I was making about $3000 USD per month, $1800 of this went to Pharma for my heart condition, birth control, and the random anti-biotic as I got sick A LOT. The rest was for living, I didn't need to pay rent to my fiancés so I looked at my expenses...car, credit card, nails, hair, alcohol...I examined where I could cut things out, so I stopped getting my nails and hair done in order to pay for 2 sessions per month with a therapist I found online. I also bought a coffee maker to make coffee at home and stopped going to Starbucks every day. This gave me more than enough for the sessions plus I could now build a savings account!

The reason I started going to therapy... was over the issue with my friend that my fiancé didn't like, which was now the 3rd friend he wanted me to separate myself from since we began our relationship...I didn't understand this. I thought I was good at making honest and kind friends, I didn't want to ask his permission for my friendships but I also didn't want to make him angry. In addition to deciding how to address my friend, and planning a wedding, my employer who had been amazing, was going through her own life crisis. Her personal life was melting down into my part of her business. I was managing more than I could at work, not getting paid for it and not getting the deserved recognition. I was beginning to be taken advantage of, yelled at yet, and manipulated and it hurt when this was a person who I thought was my friend and mentor.

Whereas in recent years work had become my solitude away from this behavior at my home when my mother-in-law was living with us, I was now receiving the same emotional abuse at work. I was seeking a therapist to help me sort out my shit because I found myself crying on the way to work, at lunch breaks, escaping to the toilet for quiet time, and crying the whole way home only to hide in my room. I was surrounded by this behavior and felt there was no escape, I was learning to cope with it all by again having too much wine every night, which wasn't helpful or a sustainable way to live. My spirit was beginning to scream at me that something was wrong, but I still wasn't listening completely, I was busy blaming myself and looking for someone to save me.

It was also at this time that I was introduced to essential oils for my emotional stability, helping me with infections, colds, migraines, etc. My best friend of the plant world, weed became a daily go-to as I was doing my best to get off of the dependency on Big Pharma and drink less alcohol. On the really tough days, I'd have a small hit before work and loads of it as soon as I walked in the door, otherwise, I'd be taking a Valium or Prozac to help me through the day. This routine I had kept up for about 10 years, not seeing the issue of dependency and coping.

I began working my way off pills, completely off by the time I entered therapy at 29, no longer taking pills that I'd taken for almost more than 10 years. I was still on birth control to manipulate my period because my ex-husband found it "gross". Another Red Flag that I again, chose not to see because his seeing me as unworthy of attention one week per month, validated my daily story of unworthiness.

I removed myself from all of the Pharma, in secret. When my family found out they were upset, telling me I needed to stay on the pills because the doctors said so...I had been living pill-free and healthier for almost 6 months when I revealed my secret. The more I stopped taking the pills, the more my eyes were opened to the red flags in my life. The more I wasn't sure how to cope with them and smoked more weed because I was seeing abuse all around me, but hadn't opened my eyes enough to put that word to it...yet. All I was knowing is that it didn't feel good and I hated crying all day long.

Following a few months of therapy, I started developing boundaries, becoming assertive, and standing in the gap for myself when for most of my life I hadn't done this, I had waited and hoped others would do it for me. I was pissing off everyone in my life....my boss because I wouldn't work hours for free and stopped putting in overtime; my fiancé because I was telling him "No"; my parents because I wasn't asking for guidance...my mother in law because I was telling her when she was out of line. I had my girlfriends in my corner and I hung on to them for life. I needed their support through my wedding preparations as I fought my future mother-inlaw on the fact that it wasn't her wedding.

The person who noticed the biggest change in me was my sister-in-law and her friends...all asking me what I was doing. I told her that I was seeing a therapist and was really starting to see life more clearly, and loving myself more. She asked for her number, and my sister-in-law and several friends went to her as well. My sister-in-law then started making dramatic changes in her life and we had one another for support as we both were making big steps for ourselves without much support from those around us. It was the first time that I began to feel what it was like to have someone support me in making my own decisions and the first person in my friend circle to point out that I had options.

I truly noticed that my life, wasn't my own when it was two weeks before my wedding and I was walking the venue with my wedding coordinator and planner...they asked me so many questions about what I wanted... "I don't know", is all I could repeat.

As the questions kept coming, I just burst into tears... "I don't know what I want because this is my fiancé's wedding...I don't know what he wants and I don't want to get it wrong." As the tears ran down my face, they stared at me, jaws on the floor...and one said, "Let's take a break."

She took me inside to make me a cup of tea, then said something to me I won't forget...I think she saw the writing on the wall but knew it wasn't her place to really call it out so she put it gently.... "Sweetheart", she began, "You live your life for you. If others around you tell you what you want and you follow them, how will you know what you like or what you want? This is more than just seat placements...you can make these decisions for yourself it's okay to do that."

I sat there, tears rolling down my face and sipping my tea, not saying a word, absorbing all she was saying. Waves of emotions washed over me I felt embarrassed that this was the first time I'd ever considered making decisions for myself without consulting anyone around me. I wanted to hide away from the looks of pity on their faces, recognizing this, they shifted their perspective from me to one another and changed the subject amongst themselves, letting me have a few quiet moments to myself.

I asked myself, "Is marrying him even the right thing to do"? Then quickly pushed it out of my mind... "It was too late," I thought...I was already committed and needed to follow through with my commitments, "Changing my mind isn't an option, everyone would be so mad at me." I brought my attention back to the room as I quickly shoved down the thoughts of about and the questions coming up, that if I answered honestly would totally blow up my life. I wasn't ready or willing to look at myself or my life, so I did what any good Texas girl would do, sweep it under the rug and move my mental furniture around to not see it anymore.

She then asked, "If you had your dream wedding what would it be?"

I replied, "On the beach, with bare feet and just a few people."

She said, "Okay well you're in the city so let's work with that. What are your favorite things in nature?"

"Trees" I replied.

The venue had a beautiful tree in the courtyard and she asked, "Do you want to say your vows under the tree?"

I looked at her, tears in my eyes, yes! "That would be perfect", I replied.

"Are you sure you want to say your vows?" she asked...me

not catching her drift said, "Yes that would be nice to do it there".

"Okay", she replied, "We'll set it up this way."

When my fiancé arrived, she told him the plan, he wasn't asked many questions, they just let him know what we decided and why. She spoke for me and asked questions directly to me...I didn't see what was happening at the moment but she did.

This is what happens when someone has been emotionally abused or controlled for so long, they don't know what they want, how they want it or what to say. We can be emotionally abused by others around us or by ourselves for many years, which breaks the spirit down into deep feelings of unworthiness, uncertainty, or insecurity.

I needed an ego boost, I needed someone to stand in the gap for me because at the time, no one was and I didn't see my situation. My spirit knew...I cried a lot, there were a lot of fights...I uninvited people to the wedding and broke up friendships...thinking I was doing the right thing.

I had been taught by my religion that this is what a woman does for her husband, give him whatever he wants and is praised for sacrificing herself. At every sacrifice, I knew what I was doing, I knew I was denying myself my needs or desires but I thought I would be rewarded or loved more for it. This is how I was taught and trained to be and I was really good at it, to my own detriment.

I think looking back many people could see this but like I said, it was the environment and so while they made faces, and small comments here and there...they were all in similar situations with their partner, parents, or employers so they also didn't know what to do or how to manage the situation. We were each doing our best with the programming that we'd been given, and up to this point, no one had the courage to step outside of the program to clear the pattern.

COURAGE TO FOLLOW INTUITION

It took courage for me to begin to walk away over and over from these abusive patterns that I didn't realize had been developing and engrained in me from my environment. It took my therapist to point out to me the intuition that I held that I was choosing to ignore because the same environment had told me I was crazy to listen to it...while also telling me to listen to it... but it was their voice they wanted me to hear, not my own.

Sometimes it's like that, the voice of intuition is a voice that almost speaks a foreign language. It talks and talks and talks but we don't understand what it's saying when we only know another language, that isn't our own. Then we begin to listen just enough to hear it communicating but we don't comprehend it, we doubt and second guess. It's now speaking on the same wavelength but it's using words and context that's coming from another time, another generation...we're listening but with a very confused look on our face.

Then over time, the confused look fades...and the language may still be hard to decipher but the energy is more recogniz-able...sometimes you just click and in those moments is pure bliss! It doesn't even matter that most of the time you're not in sync because in this moment you are.

It only makes you want to get to know this language even more. Because now enough time has passed where the energy is lining up and the voice is sounding so familiar. It no longer sounds like your parent, your friends, your partner, someone on social media, or even your therapist..it sounds like you.

And holy shit do you have a lot to say!! So you listen. You take time and space from people and when they ask questions at first you make excuses...you're tired, busy, have a head-ache... but really you're just chillin' with you. Listening and talking to yourself...finding yourself doing and saying new things that are fun and exciting.

Then another click happens and this one hits hard.

You begin to see as you listen to yourself...you hear it tell you all the times you denied yourself of your needs...the times you said cruel things to yourself out of fear or judgment...the times you've abounded yourself in order to receive love or connection...and you breathe. As a new line of vision opens up completely to see your beauty and your pain...then you can choose.

You can embrace the pain, sit with the emotions and allow the waves of sorrow to wash over you. You can find ways to soothe and sometimes cope or self-medicate through the depths of despair...You can find new ways to love and be compassionate with yourself.

Or

You can push it down. Ignore yourself even more. Avoid eye contact when you look in the mirror because each time brings a tightness to the chest or your vision gets blurry...You can numb and suppress the pain only to perpetuate the cycle.

You may not know it yet but the choice is yours. It's always yours and you may not realize the weight of your decision in this moment...because you may not also realize that you can always shift it.

So you make your choice and you either stay in the cycle or you walk away.

THE TASK TO MAKE THE MOVE

Getting out of your comfort zone and letting go of a cycle that you've been living in, IS NOT EASY!! I don't want to imply that it is to anyone, we each circulate within stories and mindsets that keep us locked into one way of being. In my years of life, I can see so many times where I knowingly or unknowingly stayed in an unhealthy mindset because I was too afraid of the unknown to be able to step out of the shit I knew. So this is where I love incorporating more joy in my journey. Some transitional phases are very challenging and the only way to find the balance is to appreciate and be grateful for the light and the dark of the journey.

The dark being that you're In or h"ve b'en In an emotionally abusive relationship in some form or fashion. Be that with yourself, a partner, family members, employers, etc. all dynamics have the power to shift, but it's like envisioning Dorthy in the Wizard of Oz... you HAVE TO believe in yourself that you can make the shifts. To do that there needs to be a balance, of being joyful and happy during and following those moments where you've pushed way past your comfort zone and into being truthful with the current way of being that you're living in.

These moments of truth bring waves of emotions that can be hard to process, leading you to repeat the pattern and not try out something new...so I encourage you through this exercise to set yourself up for success, start as easy as need be, but START.

***

Here are two methods that helped me tremendously to keep moving forward more and more out of my comfort zone and begin listening to my intuition:

MIRROR WORK:

Mirror work is a powerful and very delicate practice when coming out of your comfort zone to begin listening to your own needs, hearing your voice, and comforting yourself. Make the commitment to do this daily for the next three weeks or longer if that feels strong. Allow time and space for the exercise to evolve slowly, there's no rush, go at your own pace and begin to make this a habit.

Begin: If you've never done mirror work before then I'll start by telling you it can be emotional at times, while it can also be empowering at others. When you're leaving an emotionally abusive cycle it's important to understand that your emotions are delicate, you might be more defensive than usual or more easily triggered in other ways. So stay soft and be easy every day.

There are many of us who have been emotionally abusive to ourselves, so you need to take the time to build trust and confidence within yourself again. Think of this when meeting a new person. You might not immediately trust them with everything correct? You need to take time to get to know them, develop something stronger, and let it evolve before complete trust is given. The same goes for the relationship with yourself.

We tend to rush through things in life which doesn't make much of a long-lasting impact on the self. Set this to be a lifestyle change, not just something you do for the week when leaving this pattern.

For the first 5 days or week (or longer if needed), just stand or sit in front of the mirror, comfortable and clothed, and just look at yourself. Maybe if feels good to look around, to study parts of your body, or your face...your goal is working to look yourself in the eye.

Set a 5-minute timer...when the timer goes off, you're done, no need to push or force.

For another 5 days or a week, set the timer for three minutes, then work up to seven minutes. This time look at yourself in the eyes...no words need to be said, just a look. Emotions will come up, allow this to happen without judgment, if you need to remind yourself, write on a sticky note on the mirror, "I WILL NOT JUDGE YOU".

For another 5 days or a week, no need to set a timer, look at yourself in the mirror and say one to three things nice about yourself. This can be about your appearance (something you cannot easily change), or about your personality, your laugh, your gardening skills...say anything that's a compliment to yourself. And SMILE! I know when you've been told by society to "Smile" then doing this on command is annoying but smile, it helps the happiness to start taking root and the judgment to clear out.

If a compliment feels a bit weird, then just smile at yourself.

Allow this process over time to take over for itself, compliment parts of your body that you haven't always liked, or acknowledge parts about yourself that you keep hidden from others. The intention behind this exercise is to begin to feel a sense of self-worthiness through your own words and eyes. The DNA codes of unworthiness and emotionally abusive patterns will melt away over time, having less and less power over you.

This leads me to the Second suggested exercise:

HAVE FUN!!

You're working on leaving deep emotional wounds and patterns behind so don't forget to find that balance for fun as you're finding the balance of more love and compassion for yourself.

FUN TIMES:

Make a list of all the things you'd love to do for fun, and

make the sky the limit...if money weren't an object or time or constraint of any kind...just make the for-fun list.

Then work backward, consider your restrictions, money, time, etc. and create lists based on what you can begin doing on your own, for free, after you save, or with friends...and get started doing fun things, outside your comfort zone, off your list.

For example: When I began this I had never eaten dinner alone at a restaurant before...I wanted to travel the world and thought, "Well, I at least need to be comfortable eating alone." So I began there, I then went to shows alone, then weekend trips within my state alone, then out of state, then out of the country...I worked myself, my courage, and my confidence up to my bigger items. I worked within the parameters of my nervous system, rather than throwing myself in the deep end.

Now you may very well be the type to throw yourself into the deep end and be successful, that's amazing!! If that's the case, then go for it! I do however always like to say it's better to crawl, then walk, then run, it ensures a longer term for success. Because it becomes your way of being rather than just getting a "quick fix" of adrenaline and then back to the same patterns.

These are steps that may already be strong within you and by revising them, you can strengthen yourself and grow even deeper. Have fun finding joy in your journey! Have fun finding the balance as you make the choice to get out of your comfort zone.

4

Overcoming Shame
Through Vulnerability

Shame and vulnerability go hand in hand when on a healing journey, especially when it comes to healing from a toxic relationship. In order to move through the shame, you'll need to be more vulnerable and in order to learn to be vulnerable, you'll need to move through the shame. Envision the two hand in hand, skipping circles around you, both calling for your attention and you doing all you can to ignore them...this is how society treats these two valuable emotional states.

The thing is: We all feel shame and we all have difficulty with being vulnerable, each to varying degrees within ourselves. Sometimes we say we want to be vulnerable but when the moment comes we freeze because the shame becomes louder, and we stay quiet, choking on our shame and telling ourselves that being vulnerable is hard. The shame can be those cringy feelings of fear of rejection; fear of being reprimanded or misunderstood; the need to defend oneself; and insecurity around asking or receiving...we all carry deep shame stories that inevitably keep us stuck in a pattern.

Learning to create space for yourself to be able to dance with this duo, is a skill that you will grow to deeply appreciate within yourself. One that you can step into a leadership role for others around you, especially if you have children (if that's a choice for you) as you work through this healing work. Children are beautiful in this sense, they don't yet hold a lot of shame and when taught that it's okay to express their emotions, say how they feel, and voice their needs, they jump right into it for a chance to be seen. This is what you're doing for yourself, giving an opportunity to yourself to be seen and heard by you and by others. Overcoming shame through vulnerability is a hard step to take, so be gentle, be patient, and accept where you are; acceptance is one of the first steps to overcoming just about anything.

I've found it easier over the years to step into this role by being vulnerable with myself first, if I could admit to myself my needs, desires, and pain then it became less scary to admit to others. By that point, I didn't care about their response, I was only in the market to help myself feel good, and therefore I came into an inner knowing that if someone tried to shame me, that was on them. Sure it still hurt, but not as bad as if I was already shaming myself.

I am a person who has held a lot of shame, from an early

age, an emotional state that was there long before me, so I was carrying shame that was generational and had nothing to do with me, yet helped shape my perspective in life. So learning this skill took me many years to overcome the shame when being vulnerable, while honesty came more easily to me. I was more easily able to be honest with myself than with others because I would hide behind the mask of shame. It wasn't until I began really deep work on myself that I was able to move through both.

There are times in your life when there are people who are safer for this exercise and growth step than others who may be around you. I had some friends who no matter the topic were just not safe spaces to be vulnerable with, they would turn it around on me or use it against me at a later date. It probably goes without saying, that these people quickly exited my life once I realized their own pattern and unwillingness to be vulnerable was hindering our friendship. Then there were people who were safe spaces for this growth, allowing for the emotions and vulnerability because even if it made them uncomfortable, they were okay with the discomfort through love for themselves and me. Know your audience, this will only come with the courage to open up.

When you begin this work there often come scenarios where you just feel the burning need to open up to someone, you get to talking and without realizing have completely spilled the tea, telling your whole situation and life story. Soon after this, you feel that twinge of regret... You think, "Oh God,

I shouldn't have done that! I shared too much!" Then the stories of shame that you carry flood your mind causing you to really overthink things and look for the nearest exit...this is called a "Vulnerability Hangover", it's totally normal and very real. Just like a real hangover from alcohol or too much partying you feel sick to your stomach, sweaty, headache, shaky hands...to list a few symptoms. In these moments, I just begin to take slow deep breaths, telling myself, "Even if they don't see you through this story, I see you. I'm proud you opened up. It's all going to be okay." This reassures me that I'm not only proud but acknowledge the step I took and the courage needed to open up.

Over time this reduces in frequency as you learn to decipher who to share with, what to share, and what to keep to yourself. We often mistake sharing every intimate detail or oversharing as being vulnerable or a way to connect, this isn't the case...it's simply oversharing. Some things can be kept to yourself, this is the relationship you have with yourself, and it's the trust that you build with yourself over time. Vulnerability doesn't mean sharing everything, especially if it feels really uncomfortable, share what feels nourishing to share, this also helps to decipher who to share with. Additionally, it helps you to see and accept where you are on the sharing and vulnerability meter, it takes time to develop this emotional muscle, practice, and stay patient.

We put a tremendous amount of self-imposed pressure on ourselves in order to be perfect, do it right, say it right, etc.,

etc. Notice that nine times out of ten this pressure is some type of story that you are carrying around, putting on yourself, and can cause you to freeze or remain stuck. As you move through small steps of vulnerability, you move through the shame that is the self-imposed stories. The stories of shame that you live inside will keep you locked in a pattern or cycle until you're ready and willing to break free from them and allow yourself to be honest and vulnerable with yourself.

I learned very quickly the power of vulnerability, the symptoms of a vulnerability hangover, and the weight of shame, as I learned to hold space for myself as I moved through the weight of shame that flooded over me. My brand new marriage, which never had the "Honeymoon period" was coming to an end more quickly than it began.

ON THE BRINK OF DIVORCE

Following my marriage, I quit my job to start my own business in interior design, where boundaries and holding space for myself came on very quickly! I was in charge and leading construction sites, choosing designs and colour schemes without needing to ask anyone. Through the therapy that I'd had, I'm 100% sure this prepared me to take this leap of faith in myself to branch out against the grain and go out on a limb into entrepreneurship.

I soon realized how alone I was too. The aloneness felt very vulnerable and scary. I didn't fully see myself as a professional, a leader, a business owner, or a boss babe and it all landed in insecurities...I needed external validation. I hadn't yet built the entrepreneurial muscles to fully know I got it and to be honest, it would take me almost ten more years to move through the layers of this story.

When I had the external validation though it would certainly be the boost to the ego that I needed in order to step more into the self validation role. My business quickly grew in the short year that I was operating it. I worked really hard, long workaholic hours... drinking and smoking at night, and then waking up the next morning... going to yoga, having 2-3 cups of coffee, then back to work again.

It was about seven months into my new marriage when my husband came home from work, which for him was working and part-time living overseas, and he asked me for a divorce. He had been living and working in another country for about six to eight weeks at a time, then coming home for an equal amount of time, then back overseas again. Following our marriage, his job shifted him to move back States-side full time and he wasn't excited about it...he had been drifting away for months, almost since the 3rd month of being married.

I remember telling my friend, "This isn't going to end well, I can feel it." She assured me all was going to be okay, and that I was just being paranoid. This was told to me a lot! Anytime I voiced my intuition to someone I was either paranoid, living in fear, or too trusting...then the intuition would come true and I'd be teased for thinking I knew beforehand. This was a theme throughout my life so doubting myself was my only way of being. My mom was the only person in my life who would sometimes encourage and acknowledge the existence of intuition.

When he asked for the divorce, of course, I told him, "No!" And went about my day thinking he was just sad about his new job move and needed something to change. I was deep in denial, choosing to not see the red flag with this one, when a spouse asks for a divorce, it's a serious statement. I didn't take it as such, I couldn't bear the thought and assumed if I'd just avoided the situation, it would go away. Almost like a child who closes their eyes and thinks you can't see them because they can't see you. I was closing my eyes to what was right in front of my face and had been standing there a long time, but since I didn't want to see it, that made it "not really there".

A few weeks later he moved out. No matter how tightly my eyes were closed, it wasn't going away, I had to face the issues at hand. Not knowing that the next six months of my life would be heavily governed by the big elephant of shame that had just walked into the room and taken a dump on my new custom-fabricated rug. I was going to ignore that bad boy as long as I could...I wasn't ready or willing to deal with it. I'll just light some candles and avoid this room for now.

I called my therapist, it was she who helped me to sit down to see, admit to myself then accept that I was in an emotionally abusive relationship with a man who was narcissistic. In addition to my mother-in-law and many more around me who were also narcissists or had narcissistic behavioral traits. I was being shown that narcissism wasn't only surrounding me at this time in my life but had been there throughout my life in various forms.

I was flabbergasted... How did I not see this before? How could I have been so blind? So naive?

The answer was simple, I didn't see it before, because it was what I knew in my experience of life, which caused me to turn the emotional and verbal abuse back on myself. I didn't see it before now because I simply wasn't ready to admit it to myself. I then listened to my therapist who said, "You didn't see it because you didn't want to see it. You have known this environment and emotional pattern for most of your life, so of course you married into it." Being surrounded by narcissistic behavior most of my life be that in my extended family, friends, employers, babysitters, teachers, members of the church, or our very own government...narcissism, control, and manipulation have been woven into the fabric of our society.

So it's no wonder that I, along with millions of others are emotionally abusive to the self, then wind up energetically attracting other individuals who are vibrating at the same energetic wavelength...like attracts like and hurt people hurt people. There are reasons for these sayings and they are very applicable in this scenario. This pattern is a spiritual monkey on the back of millions within our society.

I now needed to acknowledge the elephant of shame who took a dump on my rug...was in cahoots with the monkey on my back of being surrounded by narcissists and having learned to cope with this reality. I was managing in survival mode rather than walking away, getting the monkey off my back, and cleaning up the shameful elephant shit. I had some serious work ahead of me because as soon as I witnessed this madness that had been in my life for many years, I was ready to get the hell out of this jungle of abuse.

I couldn't pack my bags just yet though because even though I was willing to see the pattern, I was living within another story that I could control the situation to my benefit, fix it, and it would all be okay. No one needed to know what was going on, I would "fix it".

This is when the shame got bigger. The shame elephant also took a big fat dump right in the middle of my newly re-modeled kitchen, and I just worked around it. At this point, I didn't tell anyone except my neighbor who was one of my best friends, that my husband had moved out until further notice and we were "working on things". This only came out because we had our morning coffee time and she noticed he hadn't been there, I swore her to secrecy and then we opened the wine...most nights. She too was a divorcee living home alone and took time to give me a lot of advice and the support that I desperately needed.

She became one of these safe spaces for me to be vulnerable with, expose it all, and lay it all out on the table. Not only was she good at listening but she was impeccable at leading by example of what I needed at the time. She'd been divorced a few years and worked through a lot of what I was moving through, so she had the available space to give me. Whereas my other friends were all happily, or seemingly happily married, younger than me, and or single... so she was the only person I knew who would actually be there for me and not judge. Her compassion and presence in my life during this time have put her in a special place in my heart, all these years later.

A month after moving out, my husband came back home, because I promised him I'd, "be a better wife". He had a list of things I needed to improve on and to do that would make him happy, therefore willing to come home to stay in the marriage. This was the first round of this tactic, we ultimately did this routine, two more times... Each time with more empty promises from him, more items on my to-do list as a wife, yet less love for one another. It took me a few rounds to realize that I could and would never measure up to these unrealistic expectations no matter how much I bent over backwards. I saw that I could break my back trying to make it work and it would never be enough, I was living out my internal story.

Before going through all the bullshit, at first I still didn't see this as a sign of any kind...just a reasonable thing for a spouse to request, "THIS is what you can do to make me happy because I'm not happy and it's your fault", he'd tell me. I was taught through the organized religion of Christianity that a wife honors her husband and obeys him. She doesn't question or cause drama, she just does what she can to make him happy, therefore he will always take care of her. I learned this through watching my grandparents interact. They were married for over 70 years but my grandfather expected my grandmother to bend over backward to make him happy while he brought home the money and did the "manly chores" around the house. The dynamic with me was that I did all the chores, except mowing grass, he brought home the money and I was to obey.

It's not only an antiquated way of being, it's whatever you want to call it...Narcissistic, misogynist, sexist, immature, unkind, unreasonable...all in all it's someone who is unhealed expecting those around them to take care of them as if they were children. It's a person with insecurities so deep they are unwilling and almost unable to take responsibility for their actions and the effects it has on others.

In addition to this upbringing, I was raised with the story that I needed to marry a rich man to take care of me, because of my health issues growing up, which were all medically induced...I "couldn't take care of myself and would never make it on my own." So even if the religious aspect wasn't involved, I believed to my core that I needed to do whatever this man asked because I wasn't going to make it otherwise. I had such low self-esteem through these stories floating around in my body that I did all I could to make him happy. When I look back at photos of me during this time, I can't help but become teary... My skin is so pale, it's almost colorless, I have dark circles under my eyes that I tried desperately to cover with makeup, and there's an emptiness to my eyes that to me shows no one is home. I was living in a true state of survival mode, petrified to make the wrong move and to be unloved even more. I was slowly sacrificing myself for the sake of another and the need for external validation...because I hadn't yet learned how to love and validate myself.

All that explained, have I said yet, that I STILL didn't see this as a problem?

So I'd had the abusive behavior of several employers before this, extended family members, friends growing up, and now my spouse...I was eyeballs deep in this pattern, stuck on the hamster wheel of letting myself be manipulated by a narcissist. As a child, I had no choice, but as an adult, I had the power to make radical changes. If only I'd known I had choices that I could make, it had taken a while longer for this program to really take root.

I agreed to more things to make him happy...For example, I agreed to wake up a 5 AM every morning to make him breakfast, have the house always clean, make dinner every night, and let him choose the TV watching most evenings.

When he went to bed, I also either needed to go to bed or be quiet, no TV, no phone talking, no coming home late. My life was to revolve around his schedule and his needs. I had agreed to go back in time to 1950 when housewives had no say in anything except what was on the menu for dinner.

I complied with this for barely two months...my nervous system was completely on edge. I began drinking a lot and smoking a lot of weed to cope with the permanent anxiety of making a wrong move or saying the wrong thing, Or heaven forbid making too much noise in the house. When I asked for help from him it was often met with statements like, he'd get to it or he didn't need to do that, it was all on me.

It was about this time that oil and gas in Houston dipped and all my clients had to end their projects early. I was down from six clients to one...no work also led me into deep loneliness and depression. Still not having told anyone that we were having these types of issues I was in deep isolation through the shame of what was happening. My worthiness, security, and ego, all plummeted and with it my ability to keep going...I only got out of bed to make him meals and then crawled back in...got out to clean, then back to bed or back to the bottle of alcohol. The only thing I did for myself was to take a shower, go for a swim, walk the dog, and do some yoga...only because this was a routine I'd had for many years and so not doing it felt worse. I believe this was ultimately my saving grace because while I did these things on autopilot for a while, ultimately it provided me with the quiet time to hear my spirit as it began screaming at me to, "PAY ATTENTION! HEAR ME!!"

I had only told my one friend what was going on, so around Christmas time I was at lunch with a few more friends when after a few mimosas, I spilled the beans that we were having issues and I didn't want to comply with my "good wife list" anymore. But feeling that it would make me a bad wife, I kept doing it. I wasn't sure what to do! I needed the liquid courage to be in that vulnerable space, I remember barely getting myself ready for this lunch and only went because my neighbor was driving me. I think she could see the dark circles under my eyes, the fact that I wasn't going to yoga class with her and was staying inside this mini-mansion not ever leaving except to run the necessary errands.

As I laid my heart out on the table, praying someone would hold it with care, their eyes filled with tears. Two more women spoke up about their marriage issues and how unhappy were. I felt the biggest sense of relief! I wasn't alone in my struggle. I had support from these beautiful people who were also going through their own hardships. We did the natural thing, ordered another round of cocktails and each took turns voicing their concerns, asking for advice, and staying quiet when listening.

These women became my rock in the coming months! We trauma bonded for sure, it felt so good to be seen and heard without shame and judgment but with true compassion. We took opportunities to empower one another and ourselves over many bottles of wine to gain the courage to make small shifts in our lives after each gathering. We'd follow up with one another, go on walks, have more lunches, and check in on the small goals we were setting for ourselves.

That year, in an attempt to cover our marriage struggles and my husband sleeping in a room across the house, of our large six-bedroom home...we threw our annual New Year's Eve bash/ block party. There were maybe 100 people, who had an amazing time, following New Year's Eve my husband's best friend who'd been staying with us for a few weeks, left to go back home. My husband came up to me with tears in his eyes...

"I know", I said.
"I'm sorry", he replied, "I just don't want to be married to you, I want a divorce. So I found an apartment in the city and I'm moving out tomorrow."

The next day he was gone and for most of the early part of the year. When we'd have company or family over, he'd drive out from the city to have family dinner, stay in a spare room, and leave the next morning. I still didn't open up to anyone that he'd moved out again. He was just "traveling" if someone asked, this wasn't out of the normal for his job so no one questioned it, for a while. After his friend left, something shifted for me, while he was there he knew or sensed something was off, so he was more helpful to me than usual.

At random he would just hug me or give me an encouraging word. My husband's friend was my favourite of his friends and while he was always a kind man, I could sense that he was giving extra love my way. I didn't even know I'd been so starved for these little morsels of kindness until he was gone, my husband moved out, and the house was so silent and still, I could feel it breathing.

The weight of shame that I felt was almost unbearable. I could barely finish the job of a big, and my only client left and didn't even send out my final invoice. I was behind on almost every deadline and barely showed up. The job ended and the client asked what was going on because he wanted to hire me for another project but there seemed to be something off about me. I told him that I was having personal issues, apologized, and declined the next job. I told him I could take another job in three months, I needed to take some time to myself to work on my health.

By this time my birthday was coming up in late February, and I had opened up to my sister about what was happening. I thought I could and wanted to save my marriage at this time, for many reasons.

I didn't dislike my husband, I liked him despite him not being the ideal partner for me. I appreciated him for his honesty because I could see the difficulty it was also causing within him. He was really funny, we had fun together when we partied, and he provided a very comfortable lifestyle. Up to this point he had encouraged me to be in better environments and see myself better, he tried to help me with my low self-esteem throughout the years. To top all of this off, I did not want to deal with all the shame and judgment that would come by way of a divorce…I felt like a total failure.

One thing I did learn through this experience of slowly opening up to those around me was that there was power in my vulnerability. I was able to see that the shame that was there was something that I had created, through the lens of my upbringing in the Christian church and my fear of "being wrong", I learned that I wasn't alone.

When we find the courage to be vulnerable about what we're struggling with, what we need, or how we feel, more often than not we discover that someone is also struggling too, we all have struggles in various forms. We all wear masks of allure to help ourselves cope with the struggle we're in and to avoid all the questions that people ask, or the judgmental comments they tend to make.

Having the understanding that the Universe is a mirror of what we're experiencing helps. So when you're struggling or going through something, there's someone in your life in the same boat, and the Universe is mirroring back to you where you are. When you see it through the eyes of another, you see that you're not alone, the shame is only another programmed story, and that compassion for the self and for the situation can be found. Often we're quick to be compassionate and understanding of those we love but struggle to reflect that back to the self. When you can find compassion for another one in your similar struggle, it's easier to sit back and put that mirror of compassion on you.

We stay stuck and rotate through a cycle over and over because we are ashamed of where we are...we expect ourselves to be different, and we have trouble accepting where we are based on the stories we carry, in addition to the unrealistic expectations we've set for ourselves. When we're leaving emotionally abusive cycles, becoming aware of our shame stories can become the most liberating experience.

UNDERSTANDING THE POWER OF SHAME

It was at this point I started some deep work with the guidance of my therapist. We began working on my values and running through scenarios to see where I'd missed the signs and how to identify them in the future...she worked hard to get me to see that I wasn't, nor had I ever done anything wrong! That there was no shame in divorce and that these things sometimes just happen, I wasn't a failure. She helped me to see that the divorce could be a valuable lesson through the experience and we frequently reviewed what I was taking away from the situation to either not repeat or to congratulate my growth.

As we combed through the past it dawned on me all the narcissistic traits he possessed...the emotional abuse...the insecurity...the verbal abuse that was developing because he wasn't getting his way. When I'd give him his way, he'd often acknowledge it with a thank you or comment on the benefit of my decision, causing me to feel "rewarded", as if I was good and had done the right thing. I see now that this is how I was raised since a pre-teen through the Christian church and school, so I didn't know that this wasn't the way things were supposed to be. I, like many of us, was just taught through the lens of control and manipulation. So winding up in a controlling and manipulative relationship wasn't unusual, this is how the cycle perpetuates for millions of us.

When I began to understand the concept of "Gaslighting" and how it played a role in my relationship, I could see it had been there the whole time. I could recall stories from when we first began dating and it was just small or intermittent then, something I could pass off as a misunderstanding however, steadily over the years grew into the way the relationship flowed. I was being heavily gaslit and was totally unaware. Spiritually, I knew, my body would respond with an ache or illness of some kind, my mind would be confused, I would cry or have uncontrollable rage. But without having the willingness to see it, my spirit had given me all the signs for years, I just didn't want to listen, now I was ready and it was a hard pill to swallow.

So why did I want to save this marriage?

Why did I want this person in my life?

Two things, firstly, misplaced empathy in the form of pity. I felt sorry for him. I think he wanted to be a better person, he would have moments of clarity, his eyes would even change and he'd apologize for it all. He'd identify what or where he had played a role in the problem, say he didn't want to be this way, he wanted to be better and would do better. There would always be a few weeks of normalcy and healthier behaviors, then the narcissism would resurface. He couldn't help it, it was who he was, without realizing at the time that who I am as an empath was making the situation worse for us both. Together we were very toxic for one another, I enabled his behavior and he subconsciously resented me for it, only to perpetuate the patterns.

Secondly, the part I previously mentioned about abusive things being done in the name of compassion. He would tell me this often that, "He was telling me the truth" about my appearance or controlling a situation because "He loved me and he wanted to help me be a better person." I believed him until I saw this was actually manipulation and abuse in order to get what he wanted or control the situation to his benefit/comfort level.

Once I started to become more aware, I could then identify when an abusive pattern was coming, his face would look different...his eyes would almost be darker. Then he would start in on me and this would happen almost always once he spent time with his mother who carried a dark abusive energy.

She and I never got along and most of our friends wouldn't come to our house when she was there because she was so unkind. She and I argued from day one, she was a huge point of contention within our relationship, mostly because of the abusive dynamic between the two of them. One that he tried over the years to make better, ask her to go to therapy, put up boundaries, etc. he did really try, but when a child is trying to still have contact with an abusive parent it will never work. These types of people need to be in no contact unless the parent does their own deep consistent work.

This was the case with my grandfather, he was abusive when my mother was growing up and at a time in her life, she had no contact. At some point he came back into our lives because he apologized and "became a Christian", but he was still the same narcissistic person, only now he was a spiritual narcissist. He and I argued from the time I was a child, and then as I aged, I could see that he was as misogynistic to his grandchildren as he was to his children, except for the younger generation, it was "In the name of Jesus" and "What the Bible says". I argued this point with him over and over growing up...ultimately turning away from church and organized religion altogether.

Growing up I had only ever been taught physical abuse was wrong, no one had ever taught me or mentioned to me about emotional or verbal abuse, I had no idea it could be this subtle. I thought abuse was a lot of yelling and screaming or name-calling...which we didn't do, ever! My husband never called me a name and probably yelled just a handful of times in seven years. The words volatile or chaos weren't in our household at all…if anything, those traits were something I exhibited through frustration. I often look back and wonder if I'd known the signs of emotional or verbal abuse, would that have changed my experience throughout life? We were taught to look out for "bad people" who were not a part of the family, never once was it discussed that "bad people" could be within a family or relationship dynamic.

So I was not only choosing not to see the depths of this abuse, but I also didn't know the signs to look out for and how far it went for both of us, not just him towards me…I certainly wasn't a completely innocent party. Towards the end, I did a lot of reacting in those days. I had no idea how to manage my emotions because I would either keep it all in or would blow up. This is a common reaction to narcissistic abuse…hold in the emotions thinking you're being patient then blowing up at something so small because the emotions can't be ignored anymore. The biggest reason I wanted to save this marriage can be summed up in one word, shame.

I was so ashamed of what was happening:
I felt that I had failed as a wife, as a woman.
I was not a "Good Christian, so what did God think of me now?"
Was I still lovable at all?
I would "Clearly be a terrible mother and no wonder my

business and marriage was failing already one year in...I was the problem and I needed to be fixed."

The stories that came up within me came hard, fast, and strong...some days it was too much to bear which is why I was drinking and getting high, I needed coping mechanisms. At this point, it was still only my sister, a few friends, and my therapist who knew what was going on.

My therapist suggested a marriage counselor if I wanted to try to save the marriage. So I contacted three of them; at the first meeting with counselor #1, my ex didn't show up. For the second meeting with counselor #1, the counselor called my husband on his abusive behavior, causing him to walk out to wait for me by the car. This counselor told me he could help but that my husband needed to be on board, and it appeared he wasn't.

So we went to marriage counselor #2...where he didn't show up again. His excuse is that he didn't select the person, he didn't want to go to my selection because then they'll take my side. So I agreed for him to choose the counselor, and I gave him one week to book another appointment.

We met with counselor #3, he was so proud of himself for finding one, then told me, this is the last therapist he would try and then he wanted a divorce. I agreed. While meeting with therapist #3, she was asking questions and getting to know us...when she turned to me and said, "Honey, I don't know why you're here?"

"To save my marriage", I replied.

"Yes, but why? He clearly doesn't want to be here, I don't even think he loves you, he's emotionally abusive. Why will you not agree to the divorce? What are you afraid of?"

As he began to protest, she looked at him, "I'm speaking to your wife right now, let her talk", and he got quiet.

She explained to us that in her 30 years as a marriage counselor, we were only the 3rd couple she'd said this to, encouraging divorce because there was no marriage to save. She offered me help to leave if I needed it...I declined. She declined to see us again as a couple and suggested I file for divorce as soon as I was ready, this wasn't a marriage worth saving. She excused us early and on our way out, handed me her card telling me to call her anytime I needed. I reluctantly took it...asking myself, "Johnna, what are you doing? PLEASE LEAVE! It's going to be okay."

As I drove us home, he said he'd find another therapist and we could work this out, she didn't know what she was talking about. I lost it... "NO!" I remember screaming out, partly at him, partly at myself, and partly to the whole madness....I don't remember what I said but I knew it was something along the lines of, "I'm done, you can get the fuck out." I told him I would take one month to pack my belongings and find another place to live. I no longer wanted to live in our mini-mansion that I'd remodeled and lived in the past year alone, I wanted a clean break. I wanted as far away from this situation as I could possibly go. It was at this point that I couldn't pack my bags fast enough. I went home, opened a bottle of wine, walked across the street to my neighbor's house, and recounted the meeting with the therapist, asking for her divorce lawyer. I was ready and there was no changing my mind.

What finally shifted in me? I was so tired of sacrificing myself to play these games that he was playing and that I allowed to be played. I was becoming suicidal...feeling so unlovable, undesirable, and undeserving...it was slowly destroying me. My drinking was out of control yet I was hiding it from everyone...sneaking into one of the two bars to have a shot of vodka here and there was an absolute problem. I was spiraling and I was going down alone...no one knew I was struggling so heavily.

I stood back and started becoming hyper-aware of my behavior and his...when I found myself saying many times, "If you speak to our kids (hypothetical) the way you do to me, I'll kill you." I found hate growing towards him so strong that I meant these words...I would never let him speak to a child this way. Then as I became aware of this passion for a hypothetical child, why could I not give that to myself? Why am I allowing myself to be degraded, gaslit, and manipulated to the point of suicidal or even homicidal thoughts? Why do I not just let this relationship die as it was wanting to do?

At this point, being so over my own shit, I was willing to do anything to feel better and to get to WHY I was accepting this behavior. Or WHY I thought so little of myself that I would continue this cycle. What was I so afraid of if things changed, if people found out if we got a divorce? Was my shame and fear so great that I would stay in an abusive situation? How could I grow some nuts to walk out of this environment?

I was given a sign from the Universe, just the one I needed to give me that courage and one that I finally played witness to in the most unrealistic way as if I was watching it play out in a movie.

It was a few days following the decision to divorce after meeting with the 3rd counselor. I was eating a meal with my husband and his mother. She'd come over and immediately busied herself by making negative comments about the inspirational quotes all over the house that I'd written on little sticky notes. At dinner we were discussing something, I was holding my energy high as I knew this was the last meal I'd ever eat with her and I was elated...in the conversation, she turned to say something demeaning to my husband...I watched this play out like I'd never seen it before.

His head lowered, his shoulders sank and he shoveled food around his plate...my eyes widened seeing this change over her harsh words. I did what I usually do, stood up for him, and told her she was out of line...this pissed him off and he turned to me to say almost the exact same demeaning words to me that she'd spoken to him...his eyes dark and brow furrowed as he looked at me. I glanced across the table at her and could almost see a small smirk on her face at the enjoyment of my being told off by her son. She was the only person who actually enjoyed watching him do this, when he'd do it around other trusted friends or his family their eyes would widen, jaw open, and no words... they couldn't believe what they were seeing. Not her though, she subconsciously knew and took pleasure in the entertainment.

The Universe literally said, "You want a sign? Here's what the circle of abuse looks like, here's what you've been actively ignoring for years."

I was finally seeing it now, the difference was I'd been in 2 years of therapy at this point and I was not going to be belittled anymore...I sat straighter, lifted my chin, looked at him then to her where she held a faint smile...I looked back at him and smiled. "That's okay, I forgive you", was all I replied, I stood up with my plate and left the room.

I was so proud of this moment, the moment to see the abuse in action, to play witness to it, and to not sink down into it anymore. I was proud that I'd made the decision for myself to walk away and that in a matter of a few weeks, my apartment would be found and I could be out of this house for good.

This is the path I was walking...and I was ready to walk it alone if it meant that I would be happy. If it meant I would be out of the abusive environment.

I reached out to my divorcee friend, who knew what was happening, for help and she immediately flew into action to help me contact a lawyer, find an apartment, get it furnished, and of course drink wine with me.

I was so afraid to be vulnerable through the shame that I was feeling, it was causing me to sacrifice myself, my needs, my sanity, and my well-being in order to keep the status quo.

How many times in your life have you done this, sacrificing your needs in order to keep the status quo? In order to keep the questions away, or the negative remarks from others...in order to keep things going "Your Way", telling yourself that you're helping yourself when really you're causing more emotional damage?

When we're in extreme resistance this is what it looks like. The Universe had been trying to break us up for most of our relationship, but I kept going, I wouldn't let it go out of fear and shame of being a failure. So when it came time for the end, it was more painful and dramatic than it needed to be due to the fact that I resisted and was still resisting!

As soon as I agreed to a divorce, that shame elephant in the room evaporated like rain that's just hit the ground on a hot Texas afternoon...the sun came out, the birds sang and I could finally breathe again! I could breathe because the monkey on my back jumped off and ran back into the jungle without me in fear of losing the attachment. Don't get me wrong, I was scared shitless of my next steps but I had allowed this inner knowing to burst through that told me, holding up banners, waving pompoms, "IT'S ALL GOING TO BE OKAY!! YOU'LL MAKE IT THROUGH THIS!"

LIVING THROUGH SHAME

I quickly learned in the coming weeks how my life decision and my personal trauma would shame and trigger the fuck out of everyone around me. My biggest fear with telling people was: "What would they would say?" The questions they would have that I didn't want to be asked or to answer. I was afraid to be viewed as a failure.

I quickly got over this though, it suddenly shifted. Almost overnight the fears and "what ifs" immediately went away, I no longer cared what anyone would think because I knew without a shadow of a doubt that I was doing the right thing by myself and no one else.

I began going back to yoga classes daily, working out, swimming, and walking the dog in the park, I was MOVING the energy and getting all the sadness and stuckness out of my body. I eased up on my drinking, got into a regular sleep pattern, and began putting the feelers out for a part-time job, gaining an opportunity within a week's time. I was packing up and getting ready to move out into my own apartment to live alone for the first time in my life at the age of 31! It had been a little over one year since I'd been married, I was still adjusting to that life when this one was beginning to take shape.

The people who I'd always been close with and assumed would remain close began taking steps back...the shame I'd feared would crush me came down hard like a hammer. I had Christian friends tell me that from the advisement of their pastor, they couldn't be there for me because my divorce would be disruptive to their own marriage and that I needed to go to church to consult a pastor. There were other friends or family members from his side telling me that they needed to side with him and that he gets mad if they have contact with me, so they couldn't be friends anymore. Then there were my friends and family who I thought wouldn't walk out but they found the situation so triggering to their own lives that quickly, one by one they broke off our friendship or just ghosted me. I even had a few friends so triggered that I was making the move to walk away, meanwhile, they were choosing to stay in an abusive cycle of their own and therefore ended our friendship out of incompatibility.

They took the news really hard, they were used to coming to our house for parties, dinners, etc. regularly, so my life-style change was also about to change their lives as well. We were all in relationships where the men were friends and the women were even closer, the change affected our relationship and the common issue with divorce or break up, "Whom to side with?" Or "Can we still be friends with you both?" These dynamics might work short term but it all quickly dissolves over time.

I felt so much shame that I couldn't even focus on it, or tap into how it was all causing me to feel at the time. I'm a reasonable person, and I always appreciate honesty so I just chose to not let their leaving my life affect me, I had too much going on to do that. I don't fault anyone for walking away and doing what was best for themselves, did it hurt? Yes. Did I feel alone? Absolutely. But I also understood that we each need to protect our own energy or relationships when something chaotic is happening around us.

When a lot of trauma is happening at once, it's totally okay and normal to compartmentalize it or turn yourself off to it so that you can keep going. It will eventually come up to come out when you're ready to manage it, trust me...so if you do this from time to time, you're not doing anything wrong. This was exactly what I was doing, compartmentalizing to be able to manage what I could when I could and to let the rest sort itself out. I was learning to let go of control and to trust the process.

When I moved out of my ex-husband's house a lot had already changed and in the coming months was going to shift even more.

My ex-husband and I surprisingly always communicated well, the honesty was mutual, and we wanted to make this smooth for both of us. We met at a coffee shop a few months after I moved out and did just that, both explaining what we felt, why we were acting the way we were, and that we each wanted the best for the other. We came to a comfortable agreement on my alimony and sharing custody of our dog, (which only lasted one visit).

This is one thing I always appreciated about him and me as individuals, we were able to sit down to have clear conversations once the chaotic emotional dust had settled. I can see now that we both communicated well but that we didn't comprehend one another well at all, so even if narcissism wasn't involved, it may have not lasted long anyway.

My marriage to him was a relationship that came into my life to give me many lessons, to show me what karma I came here to clear, to help me overcome shame, fear, abandonment, and trust issues, and to propel me to empower myself with the worthiness that I deserve. How so many wonderful things can come from such a traumatic experience I never thought possible, it was from the determination and love that I committed to give to myself. I didn't want to live in fear and shame, however was willing to take the necessary and actionable steps to get out of those thought patterns as my "Go To" programming.

Here I was at 31, I had my own apartment for the first time

in my life! I had been saving my allowance that my husband had given me and furnished it with the extra money he gave me to get myself started.

I also had a new job opportunity for a 6-week trial, which was perfect for me. A friend hired me in his business and I was so excited to see him and work with him in his office. His girlfriend was one of my closest friends still standing by me, they were two people who I needed in my life and whose love and support of those days still make me smile almost eight years later. To this day, I jokingly say, "She's the best thing I kept from my marriage", as our friendship has been through many changes in the past twelve years.

Divorce was probably the most heartbreaking thing I've been through and a lot of shit has happened since then. I didn't only end a relationship with my husband but broke up with close to or more than twenty people. To say I was heartbroken is an understatement. At the time my coping was alcohol, weed, and yoga...I was looking at every tiny thing for the silver lining. I needed to know I was going to be okay. I needed to know that I would make it.

Due to the pain of divorce and the trauma that follows it...I wouldn't wish this experience on anyone. On the flip side of the coin, I also wouldn't, "avoid it at all costs" as an excuse to stay in an otherwise unhealthy or shitty situation, this is what I was doing in the beginning and it gradually made it worse, not better. I've known so many people to not leave these types of relationships because of, "the kids" or "We've been together so long already". These are excuses all just a fear of the unknown, a fear of blowing up your life and wondering if you'd be able to pick up the pieces. Fear of the shame that comes from the opinions of other people on the outside looking in. There are so many stories that keep one inside an abusive situation but know that you have choices even when it feels like you don't.

As I embraced my choice to leave, I was embarking into wild unknown territory...newly divorced, new apartment, with a new job, new friend who was giving me attention...most importantly, I had full faith in myself that though my life had turned upside down, I was going to make it. Things had dramatically shifted at this time, and little did I know would continue to shift as the time and years went on....leading me to sit in this café in Bali, writing this book.

The shame that I was petrified to live through was actually the very thing that liberated me from a pattern of abuse, as soon as I leaned in and stopped resisting the hard crusty shell of my whole world crumbled, and opened to reveal the vast opportunities that I had at my disposal. I then was granted a new lease on life to rebuild it however I wanted it to look.

This is what the Universe wants to show each of us! When we let go of control, stop resisting the change, and accept what's happening, even when it's not in our own plan, so many things open up to support us and show us love and care, time after time. It only takes you to accept it and let go of resistance to be able to receive the blessings.

***

MOVING THROUGH SHAME TO FIND SELF COMPASSION

Some of my biggest hangups in moving through the healing of divorce to open up to being vulnerable and let go of shame, was to find compassion and empathy for myself.

We each hold shame for various reasons, and so often aren't even aware of it. Someone can make a comment, correct something you've said, embarrass you, or make you the brunt of their joke...any of these can be reasons to feel shame. Finding compassion for yourself in these moments is important.

Bear witness to the fact that you're healing from a relationship where compassion and empathy were not present. You didn't have the support that you needed whether it was from your partner or from surrounding friends and family, this can feel lonely and make it hard to want to be vulnerable with anyone. If the vulnerability is new for you, I suggest softening towards the world around you as you move through your day. Leaving a narcissistic abusive relationship makes you grow walls and become defensive in your choices, words, or actions. This is how it was within your home life, so of course you would take this defensiveness out into the world.

Beginning to soften to yourself and the world around you, helps to let go of the shame and pain associated with it. I'll share with you an exercise that I did when I took a Brené Brown course on Shame about eight months after my divorce, it was something my mother sent to me, being hosted at my local family counseling center.

We spent eight weeks learning about shame and sharing shame stories, here are the nuggets I took away.

EXERCISE:

Who in your life can you be vulnerable with?
(This person is someone you can be yourself around, have any emotion without judgment and who supports your ideas without unwanted opinions.)

Identify this person(s) for you, tell them that you're working through this book and healing from your experience, and ask them if they are open to being a soundboard for you to practice being vulnerable. If interested and available for you, you could offer to do this for them as well and it could be a friendship effort, deepening your connection to this friend.

This approach and question alone is vulnerable, in my experience when I asked this of my friends I chose the right person because they were always open arms willing. And appreciated the opportunity to expand themselves. Each of us wants to connect deeper to ourselves and those around us, many not knowing how to even do it.

Create a space with your friend to be open, honest and

no-judgment zone, they will appreciate you seeing them as much as you need to be seen.

Write letters to strangers and yourself...I know it sounds weird but it works! :

You begin to see the world totally differently. The letter doesn't have to be mailed if you don't want to, it's about the act of energetically having compassion, empathy, and vulnerability with a stranger that assists you to develop it with yourself. Allow their story to be one that's a mirror for you in your life...connect, empathize, be honest, and be compassionate.

Why a stranger? We often feel more judged by those we're closest to, sometimes opening up to strangers is easier because there's that sense of, "never seeing them again" so less likely to be judged or care of their opinion. This is an exercise you can do with your trusted vulnerability buddy or alone, your choice.

Inside the Shame Workshop, we wrote and mailed a letter to a woman whose shame story was broadcasted across the Houston papers, being read by millions of people. The tiny details aren't important, her husband was a church member discovered having an affair with a student; they had children and he was a person who, "Nobody saw it coming".

While the details of the story are something that we as humans can get caught up in because we seek out drama by and large. The tiny details of another person's life aren't important because it's more about the emotions associated with the situation. We identified how she must be feeling...betrayed, lied to, ashamed, mortified, afraid, etc. Each of us in the course wrote a letter to her, it was a small stationary paper, empathizing with an emotion that comes from discovering your spouse has been deceitful.

Locate a story you read online, something that tugs at your heartstrings, and as you read it you get emotional. Again, don't get caught in the details of the stories, or even hung up on the trauma, or the shame of it all, focus on the emotions to empathize with. You don't need to spend hours researching it or falling down the habit hole of this particular situation, in fact, I encourage you to read ONLY ONE article that grabs you, then let it go and proceed to the assignment.

It's about finding compassion for those who were deceived in some way, not giving advice or opinions, for example, your letter would look something like this:

EXAMPLE: "I've read about your story and I wanted to say, I'm sorry this has happened to your family, I'm praying you find the support that you need through this difficult time. I know what it feels like to be deceived and how overwhelming this must be for you. Please know you are not alone, there are people you don't even know being compassionate toward your experience and wishing you peace."

This letter offers no opinions, no details of their story, and no judgment, all of that is completely irrelevant; instead, it offers empathy, a kind word, and gentle support.

Taking time to see another individual you don't know gives you space to see yourself more and let the weight of shame slowly dissolve. Making more space for love and self-compassion through the journey of healing from a painful experience in your life.

When I use the term "self-comparison", I don't want to confuse it to the act of comparing yourself to others, we are very guilty of this as a society. Comparing to others, takes energy away from you when you're comparing the details.

For example: Comparing to one another in a judgmental way causes you to lose your energy, and would look something like this:

"I'm glad I'm not her, I bet her husband does __________ or she probably should've _________. Things are bad on my end but they're not THAT bad."

We say this last phrase a lot in comparing our life to that of someone else, this comparison diminishes our experience and that of the other individual, and each of us is in no place to judge the experience of another person. They are here to clear karma and make different growth decisions as much as you are, when you judge or compare their experience you are sitting in a "better than" seat and no one should be in that seat. No one is better or less than one another on this planet, we are all unique and living different experiences, so stick to your lane and don't attach to the story, see the emotions, find the love.

Self-comparison in the sense of identifying the similarities of emotions looks something like this:

"I haven't had a cheating spouse before but I do know what it's like to feel betrayed and wonder if you could've done something better. It's none of my business what went on in their marriage, but I know she's hurting now and I hope she's able to find peace and know she's loved."

Lastly, write a letter of this style to yourself, can be past or present self...empathizing with a particular scenario that you went through or are going through in relation to emotional abuse. This can be a scenario that was self-inflicted or inflicted by someone around you. Let yourself be seen and loved completely by you...develop empathy for yourself as you are the one who deserves it the most.

In this exercise we go back through the shame emotions, we feel them, we are present with what comes up and we don't avoid it, don't shy away and don't put judgment to it, it simply is what it is. The emotional shame is there and through this exercise, you can shift the energy from shame of vulnerability to strength in yourself through being more vulnerable.

I know this is scary at first and still can be to me many years later but I believe that if we as individuals and a society can learn to be more vulnerable with one another about our fears, need to be seen, desires to be loved, and willingness to be gentle then our world would look dramatically different to how it does today.

This is the power of the karmic shift within the self. Being vulnerable steps further away from fear and manipulation and into honesty and compassion...the more we move away from fear the greater we can love and deepen the relationship to ourself.

5

Grieving & Moving Out of
Emotional Abuse

Throughout all of the changes and shifts that were happening in my mind, there was one thing that hit me like a bag of bricks...I was stunned when I looked back to see the life that I had created for myself. It was one where I had willingly and sometimes unknowingly abandoned myself in order to receive acceptance and what I thought was love. This wasn't only coming from my ex-husband, but I was looking for this from friends, family, employers, and members of the church I was going to. I was externally seeking validation and in doing so, landed myself in repeated emotionally abusive situations.

At this point in my therapy, I hadn't gotten to how I was abandoning myself in order to receive love, she was delicately pointing it out to me to notice on my own. This term wasn't yet in my vocabulary, however, I was becoming aware that if these situations were a repeat pattern, I was asking myself,

"Where did you learn this?" And making the statement to myself, "This will not happen again, I assure you."

For me, only one person in my life pre-divorce who made a hard and courageous phone call to me. When this friend called me, she voiced that she'd been seeing the pattern of emotional abuse within my relationship for a while and apologized for not saying anything sooner. She flat-out asked me to get divorced and not try to have children with him. She encouraged me to break free as soon as possible and don't look back. She was someone close to my ex-husband, and a good friend to me. She acknowledged that she would need to stay on his side following the divorce and she knew that would end our friendship. She was willing to lose me as a friend if it meant I would eventually thrive and be happy.

Her gift of honesty and hard truth sincerely gave me my life back. It gave me the courage to look at myself in the mirror, to see my physical appearance, the dark circles, the paleness of my skin and lips as the life had drained out of me. I was able to make the harder admittance to myself that, she was right...and I never saw it before now. I, like many of us in relationships, thought if I could do THAT ONE magic thing, it would all be better. I even told my friend, that if certain scenarios were different, it would be okay." I then began to list for her all the things I thought needed to change, that was basically me wanting to change a person, rather than accept the situation. "You're right", she replied, "if that wasn't a factor, it would be better. But it's not, it is what it is, and you're describing two different people, that's just not going to happen." She was so right, I knew it, I acknowledged it to her and thanked her for being so honest with me when it was hard for her to share this and put the boundary in place. That was the last time this friend and I spoke, and I thank her frequently for helping to save me.

I had thought and told myself that I needed to suffer because I believed myself to be unworthy of anything better. Many years later I know differently but I first had to accept and admit the pattern to begin to break it.

There was another area that also hit me pretty hard. Following my divorce, several of the women in my family admitted to seeing the patterns of emotional abuse, yet didn't know how to address them with me. My experience of divorce had triggered them to take note of what they didn't say and to now come forward after the fact to open up about what they had witnessed.

At the time, this really hurt me. I felt a deep sense of betrayal from my husband and now from friends and family who took a long time to speak up. After digesting this admittance I've been able to forgive them and the situation. Seeing that when people are triggered sometimes it's easier to say nothing, perhaps even walk away and in their own way ignore what's in front of them. I haven't had an in-depth conversation with anyone who came forward after the fact, it's one I never felt was needed. It shifted my perspective in many ways on how we all manage our own pain and triggers from abuse, the weight of shame can be one that causes an individual to freeze or become fearful. When we're in these states within our nervous system then it's hard to tap into the heart space to do hard things outside of the comfort zone.

However, if you have someone close to you in an abusive situation and you don't say anything, then you run the risk of assisting in the perpetual cycle of abuse. You are aiding and abiding the abuser in their manipulative tactics against the one you love and hold dear...not saying anything makes you part of the problem. I say this bluntly because it's one of those hard truths that needs to be said in such a manner in order to get across the severity of the situation. Abuse of any kind isn't something to take lightly or joke about, and least of all nothing to "look the other way" on. Our society has become so desensitized to abusive behavior that we either don't see it when it's happening to us or in front of us...or if we do, we take the victim role and say nothing out of fear. If you suspect someone you know in an abusive situation, say something!

When I asked those who came forward with their statements, WHY they never said anything to help me, the response was, "Well, I didn't think you'd listen to me."

I replied to them all; "I may not have made any changes at all. I may have still gotten married and would probably still be getting a divorce but you would have planted a seed within me. I would have felt it every time I was gaslit rather than feeling stupid, or crazy".

Choosing to stay silent doesn't help anyone, just as trying to control the situation doesn't help anyone. If you see this and it's upsetting or triggering for you, and you find yourself frozen in fear, consult a professional for help. They can assist in the best approach for you and even play mediator if the situation calls for it. In order to stop patterns of abuse we have to work together as a community to be there for one another, to go to someone in love, and to also be prepared to accept their response. You may build the courage to say something but that doesn't mean they have to or will listen, they may stay in their pattern, and it's up to you to do what's best for yourself after that. It is not your place to control the life decisions of anyone, I always suggest saying your peace once, maybe twice then leaving it to them as it's not yours to bear. You can support and love someone from a distance if they choose to remain in abusive patterns.

At this time I was furious and brokenhearted all over again. I was being told this about a year after my divorce and the weight of the grief hit me in another layer. I then decided to take a season of separation from my family, I was so overwhelmed with emotions and needed to be in my own energy in order to sort it all out. I sat in my woes, and moved through my anger...with all my coping mechanisms....I did what I do best and what comes naturally to me, I observed.

I observed the relationship that I was currently in, as at this point I was dating someone.

I observed the habit of alcohol within my life and those around me.

I observed the cycle of codependency and victimhood. I observed the stories of unworthiness, that kept strong people in fear.

I allowed my life around me to reflect back to me what I needed to shift within my life, as I wasn't here to do it for anyone else but myself.

I played witness to this in my life, with my boyfriend at the time, with my friends, my business, my past work...and I thought. Holy shit...I have been surrounded by abusive situations and narcissistic people most of my life. I wasn't alone though, so had these women who made the statement that they saw the abuse but said nothing, so were some of my friends, so were past employers...so were people I barely knew or were getting to know. I was observing that abuse, abandonment, and emotional neglect have the power to breed narcissists. Without anyone speaking out against it, the cycle and number of people involved in these scenarios was only growing in numbers.

ENDING THE REPEAT PATTERN OF EMOTIONAL ABUSE

In the year that followed my divorce, I had played the

observer to every relationship I had, both old and new...while also observing them within their life. I was not only witnessing my patterns but also seeing that of friends and family.

Seeing that narcissistic abuse played out in many of the relationships around me was jarring, to say the least. I was so confused about how this happened and also questioned, was the whole world this way? Was everyone in some type of abusive relationship because even my new friends had their own experiences with this from time to time?

At this time, I was questioning how my life, characters on TV, and book characters, were all experiencing some type of abuse, manipulation, or another of the 7 Deadly Sins. How did we get here as a society let alone individuals?

Almost a decade later of doing this deep work I see that it is everywhere...it is a programming of our society. To be insecure, to grow entitlement and grandiose personality traits through insecurities developed in childhood or passed down through generations. To manipulate and control the situation around us in order to be comfortable, to feel safe or secure. We do this because we lack a sense of security in the body that's so deep we manipulate our external world to develop a false sense of security. We're programmed to believe that we don't deserve better, that better isn't available to us it's only available to some, and we are programmed to play small and submit. It's no wonder so many of us end up either the abuser or the abused... it's not only in the DNA but in the narrative of entertainment and society as a whole.

So to break the cycle of abuse means to CHOOSE TO BE greater than your environment, and the willingness to do so. It's the choice to break from all that you know, in order to break the cycle...it's the choice to walk or run away and recreate, reprogram yourself to be different, to live differently, dress differently, move and operate your life differently...and to heal on a DNA level. This is how the cycle of abuse is truly broken out of the generations, and out of the collective. I've grown to see that we as individuals aren't broken, it's our societal setup that's broken, which is keeping us living in these patterns as a whole. Once we make the committed choice to change, then those around us change and it ripples throughout each of us.

It's said that it takes up to seven generations to clear a pattern within a family, when you choose to do deep work on yourself, you can quantum leap this process eliminating the longevity of the pattern for the generations behind you. I figure with the work that I've done in the past eight years, deeper in the past four, I can see in the energy of my niece and nephew that much of this cycle is shifting out. My prayer and intention with my work is that they won't know abuse...they will have their own work to do in this realm as many still will but I pray it isn't as deep and doesn't affect them for life.

I wish I could say that after my divorce I was no longer in abusive relationships, but that's not true, in the year following my divorce, my boyfriend at the time and I were quickly sliding down to one of these types of relationships... So it didn't make complete sense to me and I didn't want to let go either, we were attached to one another, and neither of us could let go of the other one. Yet as the weeks rolled by emotional outbursts were happening more and more on the verbally abusive scale. With me sobbing, screaming, throwing things, and acting all out "crazy" through my rage.

It occurred to me that this situation was never going to change with him, no matter how badly I wished it would. The more I unattached myself from him, the clearer I could see. The more I stepped back from the situation we were in, stopped answering the phone, or stopped feeling anxious when I didn't hear from him...Then I could see I was setting myself up for another abusive pattern should I choose to stay in this relationship.

At this time I was getting off birth control, after having been on it for almost 15 years. I wasn't aware then, that the chemicals in the birth control tablet, shot, patch....whatever it is... throw your hormones so out of balance that you are attracted to THE WRONG TYPE OF MAN!** You are by default attracted to personality types and often end up in these cycles that you were introduced to as a child. I'm not saying this is the case for everyone involved in this dynamic but enough women find themselves in this situation that it's now a scientific study to prove patterns of women dramatically change both on and off Birth Control.

One reason that this can occur is your scent. Women who are taking Birth Control and choose a partner often become unattracted to this partner after getting off Birth Control and more than likely end up in divorce. Rather than women who choose a partner when not taking Birth Control take more time to choose a partner and choose one whose scent is unlike their own genetic makeup. This makes complete sense to me! I was once in a speed dating meet-up, hosted in a Tantric style where we were all learning the power of a hug or eye gazing. There were certain men who upon looking at them I found attractive but when it came to a hug, some of them smelled putrid. One man smelled so heavy of metals that I had to hold my breath... and it dawned on me that I would choose a partner based on his smell. When I attended this event I had been off Birth Control for six years and spent time detoxing it out of my system, so I trust my nose more these days.

When you relieve your body of the birth control hormones, it can take years for your body to regulate itself and your hormones to find their ideal balance. Years! So at this point of seeing all of this, I was about two years off of birth control and four years off many of the Big Pharma pills I was on since I was a teenager. My whole system was readjusting and I wasn't any the wiser as to what was happening, I just thought there was something wrong with me.

I see now that the man whom I was dating was someone with whom I had a soul contract. We were under the impression that it was soul mates or something equally as deep and longlasting, but our soul contract was here to teach us each a lesson. One for us to overcome, and triumph through, then move on from one another, not stay in each other's lives forever.

This is the case with many relationships that go past their expiration date. The notion of love, soul mates, etc. keeps them hanging on when it's past time to throw in the towel and lovingly walk away from one another. I didn't get that opportunity with him. The end of our relationship was a volatile one.

The "beginning of the end" started when I became aware of his ex who'd begun pervasively contacting me across multiple means of communication. One attempt, to get me fired from my job, where I still worked with my boyfriend, escalated when one of her friends contacted me as well to echo her message. All to tell me he promised her (the ex) that he'd marry her and take care of her children. My response was the same with every email or text she sent; "HAVE HIM! I don't want any part of this, your issue is with him, not me. And if you feel so insecure as to harass his current girlfriend then you need more help than a new husband."

After a few months of this, I looked over my shoulder every time I walked outside, paranoid beyond words because I was a homeowner with an online business. In Texas one can research and easily find the name and address of any homeowner, I began living in extreme fear. Furthermore with the situation escalating to him and I speculating her of pretty serious criminal offenses; I told him, that if I heard from her again I'd be filing a harassment lawsuit and a restraining order...he begged me not to do that as to now acknowledge to me...she already had this filed against her. If I filed one, it would cause her children to be taken away by the state; my response was, "That's not my problem, if she's so concerned for her children then she needs to lose my number." I was protecting myself at all costs, and in this scenario not welcoming in compassion for someone who was crossing boundaries, to say the least.

Thankfully this stopped her from reaching out as far as I could tell. I'd blocked her and the friends so I could take the necessary steps to get myself back in order. Until one day he called me to tell me that his truck, which had been in the shop had the break lines cut...and that before it went into the shop, someone broke into his truck and stole only his gun.

It dawned on me a few weeks following this event that every time I would leave the house to walk my dog, about eight times per day...I would pause at the door, hand on the handle, and say, "Today isn't the day." Take a deep breath, open the door, and step outside. I was petrified she would be there with the suspected stolen gun. I had no idea if this woman was capable of such violence but I had no desire to find out.

Every time I walked outside no one was there...then one

night I opened the door to a car I didn't recognize parked in front of my condo. I lived in a condo complex so this wasn't too out of the ordinary, it had just been quiet for so long that it caught me off guard. A man was leaning against the car, facing my house and when I stepped on the porch, he looked up to stare at me. An empty, blank stare, as if he was looking past me and not registering that I was standing there, while also staring directly into my eyes. I froze. My dog caught on her leash and the slight jerk forward didn't make me budge...then he said, "You okay ma'am?" And I shifted...I let go of the fear that had frozen me.

I had seen this guy before, he was a friend of my neighbors, he had a phone in his hand, nothing more. "Oh yeah". I replied, "Sorry, I thought you were someone else that I didn't want to see. How are you?" I laughed, and he laughed...said he was good. Then got called over to his friend's place, and he jogged off.

It was at this time as I stood on the porch, watching him go off to my neighbor's house that I heard a voice say, "You need to get your shit and get the fuck out!!!" Then the voice screamed. "GET THE FUCK OUT OF HERE! LEAVE TEXAS."

That night, I got proper "white girl wasted" by myself. Stayed up all night looking out the window...falling asleep as the sun came up and refusing to walk my dog anymore. She protested my choice but I refused her. I made an excuse and asked my parents to take my dog for a few days so I didn't need to leave so often.

I took a day trip to the five-hour drive to knock on my boyfriend's door...sit him down, tell him he needed to fix his shit, and get this crazy ex out of his life. He needed to do a lot of things because this was mostly over, I was hoping he'd get it together but he was still so attached to this abusive relationship with his ex, that he didn't. A few weeks later, he yelled at me over the phone for a simple misunderstanding. I let him finish and as soon as he took a breath he said, "And now you'll not talk to me anymore."

"That's right I replied. This is 100% over and I don't want you to ever contact me again. I did not leave an emotionally abusive marriage in order to get into another abusive relationship, you need to figure your shit out without me." He apologized. I hung up. I spoke to him months later, to learn that he hadn't made any changes in his life and that things crumbled around him as he was refusing to get help or budge out of his patterns.

After that relationship and realization, the grief settled in and began to be released from my body. All the while that voice kept saying, GET THE FUCK OUT OF HERE!!

A close friend of mine came over and cried with me, she acknowledged that this wasn't me and I needed something powerful to help me shift out of the depression. At her suggestion, I went to a Reiki session, something very new to me. I walked into the session looking like a ghost, feeling like a shell of a human but walked out feeling like a whole new me! While there the Reiki practitioner started telling me a story of a friend who..went to Bali. I don't remember the story I was just paying attention to my body's reaction to this word....I got goosebumps, all the hairs on my arms stood up, and I started tearing up...I couldn't wait to get home to research Bali. A place I'd wanted to go to years ago but my husband said no...and now this island was clearing sending me a message, "Come".

After leaving the Reiki studio, I immediately called the same friend, who then suggested that I do Yoga Teacher Training. She followed her suggestion with a story of her Yoga Teacher Training teacher, who...went to Bali.

On the way home, I stopped in the market for food, and the magazine at the checkout stand said...BALI.

"OKAY! I GET IT, Universe, message received." Giggling to myself in line the cashier said, "Oh you're having a good day!" I smiled and replied, "I think I'm going to Bali." She gushed at the idea of overseas travel as it's not a common thing for Americans. We talked about how cool it would be and she asked me to report back. I saw her weekly so while we weren't friends we knew one another's faces.

I went home, opened my laptop, poured a glass of wine,

and started researching Bali. Everything was saying, "GO HERE!! GO! GO! GO!" I got more and more excited the more articles I read and the flight tickets I saw... "What did I have to lose? Could I actually do this??" Questions were flying around in my head and I closed the computer to let it all settle in...to check in with my body to see how it felt. I would give it some time and careful consideration but all things were definitely pointing to a "Hell Yes!"

I had been in a certain level of resistance through these relationships, that I was no longer willing to be a participant in, I was ready for change. This is what the Universe does for every one of us...when we refuse to heal, refuse to follow our soul's promise for this lifetime, then our surroundings become miserable, we become so out of alignment that we look around one day and don't recognize who we are or the life we're living. The state of resistance can either be your tormentor if you choose to resist to try and do it your way, or you can let go, and find a way to break the cycle...then the suffering releases and you can breathe again.

You then look around again, not recognizing your life but seeing that it's one that you created through courage, determination, love, and compassion for yourself. It always opens up opportunities, people, and experiences that you can only respond with one statement, "I can't make this shit up and it's real!!"

MOVING THROUGH GRIEF INTO ACCEPTANCE

Anytime we have a major life shift there will always be some grief involved. Whether the shift is wanted or not, happy or not, eventually the grief will come and settle in. In order to make space to breathe, you have to process and move through the grief. Grief settles in the lungs, constricting our air supply, and causing us to have issues with the lungs or difficulty breathing, taking deep breaths, or breathing with the chest rather than with the belly.

I was moving into a space of accepting the emotional weight I had been carrying, not only of the divorce but that I was a changed person. I was still trying to squeeze myself into the mold of who I had been and I was ignoring myself on a deep level, how deep I didn't acknowledge for several more years. I was in a stage of just being aware, being aware, and accepting that I was deeply grieving; my divorce hurt me; my family and friends who were no longer a phone call away left an empty space in my heart; the loss of 'what was' burdened me; the intuition that my boyfriend wasn't my forever person, caused a longing for a partner that I wasn't ready to be with. I wanted something solid, but it was my time to float and I had come to a point of accepting it all, becoming aware, and letting the seed take root.

Grief is a funny thing, as it comes in waves. It's something that we all move through multiple times in our life, through many life changes, i.e. Changing jobs or career paths, relocating to other cities or parts of the world, healing ourselves and letting go of old patterns, and becoming who we are. These all cause grief to swell up and unfortunately, it isn't something we understand as a society, so therefore we don't give ourselves room to grieve. We don't allow the waves of emotions to wash over us, we just continue going, pushing through, and adding distractions or coping mechanisms.

If as a society we could understand and accept what's happening to us, then we would be okay to give space to the emotions. Whereas instead, we shame ourselves and one another for "not moving on" when half the time we don't even know we're still hanging on to old shit, to move on from.

If you look at the stages of grief, you can see how it manifests in life:

<u>Denial:</u>

Can Look like avoidance, procrastination, forgetfulness, distraction, busy all the time.

Can feel like: numbness, confusion, shutting down.

Manifests in the Spleen, causing the body to have an increased risk of infection, or frequently getting sick.

Also within the small intestines, it shows up as IBS, poor digestion, bacterial infections, and parasites.

<u>Affirmations:</u>

I love and accept myself.

I trust in the process.

I am safe.

I am safe.

I am safe.

<u>Anger:</u>
Can look like increased alcohol use, aggression or passive-aggressive, pessimism, sarcasm

Can feel like: out of control, frustrated, embarrassed, impatient, and resentment

Can manifest in the gallbladder, causing the body gas, nausea, discomfort after meals, and gallstones.

Can also manifest in the liver, the liver filters everything put in or on the body, or potential loss of appetite, or overall sluggishness.

Affirmation:
There is joy when I release the past.
Love, peace, and joy are with me.

<u>Bargaining:</u>
Can look like judgment, perfectionism, comparison, worrying, ruminating, assuming the worst

Can feel like insecurity, anxiety, shame, guilt, blame

Can manifest in the stomach, causing food intolerances or cravings, digestive issues, tired after meals, or any skin-related irritations.

Affirmation:
I love and accept myself.
I accept things in my life as they are.
I am safe.
I am safe.

I am safe.

<u>Depression:</u>
Can look like a reduction of energy or motivation, crying, increased alcohol use, sleep & appetite changes

Can feel like overwhelm, sadness, despair, helpless, hopeless, or disappointment.

Can manifest in the kidneys, causing fatigue, urination issues, dehydration, issues with sleeping.

<u>*Affirmation:*</u>

The Divine is working FOR me in my life, even when I cannot see it.

Only good comes from each experience that I go through. It is safe to grow and expand.

<u>Acceptance:</u>
Can look like: mindfulness, being present, "it is what it is", vulnerable & tolerant of emotions

Can feel like: good enough, validation, courageous, self-compassion

Note: can also cause a joyous and fulfilled life perspective!

<u>*Affirmation:*</u>

I accept life as it comes.
The Universe supports me.
I choose to be present as my life unfolds.

Each of these examples given is just the tip of the iceberg of moving through grief, and each one ebbs and flows. There's no phase order or time frame, no expected expiry date for each phase, and no pinpointing when it will set in. Moving through grief to find acceptance is the epitome of "going with the flow" and accepting each experience as it is.

When you leave the cycle of emotional abuse, you are leaving behind a way of being and a pattern that's deeply rooted. While, yes, leaving this behind will benefit your life exponentially, your current way of being will be naturally grieved. You are making room through your grief for your spirit to let you know that it's going to be okay, that no matter how long or how painful each phase of grief is, you will be there for you. Others will fall away, a lifestyle will be lost, change is happening, and it's scary to come into a new phase of who you are without this pattern. Finding acceptance comes more and more as you find safety for yourself.

If you noticed almost all of the affirmations it mentions finding safety in the body and trusting in the process of life. This is easier to write and easier to say than to put into practice but I can assure you it's so worth it and so doable.

It is important to remember that you're reprogramming your body, your mind, and your spirit to believe that you are going to make it! To believe that you can find trust again after having it broken by your partner and also by yourself is one reason why there's no sense of safety in the body. When you break trust with yourself as an adult, you find it hard to trust others, so when others break trust with you then it's a whole other level to find it again. So I'll repeat myself when I say, it's doable and it's a practice but will become your new way of being should you choose to stick to it with yourself.

This is when I began to truly find safety in my body by making radical changes in my life, which began with boundaries, as I'll discuss more in another chapter. The boundaries helped me to develop trust within myself because I'd set personal boundaries and then follow through with them. If I didn't follow through with the boundary, then I'd only have myself to blame, so in turn it slowly helped me to begin taking all kinds of responsibility for myself and my actions. I liked how it felt when I followed through, it built trust in myself where it had been broken and that allowed me to learn to love myself more and more.

Then I took the time and had the courage and willingness to step back to be an observer, again. I encourage you to allow the world and those around you to become a mirror for how you live your life or how they live theirs, not in a form of judgment or comparison, but in a form of, "Does this or that work for me long term?"

Be honest and get serious. Then decide if you want to make a shift or not, it's always your choice. At the very least, being aware of yourself helps you to hold more responsibility for yourself and your actions, which coping mechanisms tend to take away.

When you're grieving and doing your best to navigate

through a new way of existing, it's imperative that you take the time you need to nourish yourself first and foremost, afterwards everything else will fall into place. You've just or are about to uproot everything in order to save yourself and perhaps your children. Be gentle with yourself through this process...In order to do this, it helps me to envision the process of building a home.

For many years I worked in custom home building and interior design...in the spiritual realm the "Home" represents your body, including the rooms, the structure, and the decor...all are aspects and pieces of your body and life. So when you're leaving an abusive relationship and pattern, your home is torn down, as if someone came in with a bulldozer, you hear loud beeping sounds, then crashes over and over, as the glass shatters, the roof caves in, the walls crumble. The weight of this is so powerful and painful that you're often brought to your knees and need some way to cope, a way to deal with or manage all that's happening, this is natural.

It's normal because we haven't been taught the tools to use and even if you have them, sometimes during the dark night of the soul, the tools don't always work. Why? Because you need to feel it. You need to be aware and just accept it. Accept it for what it is, how it is, and that it is. The emotions and the process cannot be bypassed into feeling better without feeling the pain. Just like you can't build a house and leave out the windows, or have an unfinished roof...there's a process of building the plumbing, foundation, framing, roof, electric, sheetrock, floors…you get the picture. You can't bypass any steps when building a home just like you can't bypass any steps when rebuilding your spiritual and physical "Home" in the body.

Beginning to adopt the phrase, "It is what it is" assists you in bringing in more and more acceptance into your life on a daily basis.

It is what it is that "The house" got swept away by a tornado.

It is what it is that now there's work to be done in order to clear the rubble.

It is what it is that the house will slowly be rebuilt. You cannot build a home in the day, once the rubble is cleared, the foundation checked and solidified, you can begin the process.

It is what it is that the rebuilding phase takes a while. It takes patience, compassion, understanding, and acceptance of the flow.

It is what it is that over time you might not even recognize the changes you've made and how positively it's impacted your life.

You want to give yourself the time and space to do this because you need to build a strong foundation within yourself. It is what it is that as you move through your grief you will become a different person. You will walk, talk, and look different…this is part of the spiritual growth and rebuilding of that "Home". I know if you stick to it, don't run away, don't hide, and don't bypass your grief, you will move through it with strength and tenacity for the future you're creating.

By acknowledging yourself and making space for your grief you are beginning to build safety within the body, combined with a deep level of compassion for yourself and all that you're struggling with. Allow this space of grief to be an ebb and flow as you leave emotionally abusive patterns. So much will come up for you, and grief will be one of the hardest pieces to move through but I know that you can do this. You can meet yourself in your grief with love and acceptance to stay out of the pattern.

***

<u>ACTIONABLE EXERCISE:</u>

Make Space & Build Safety in the Body

My encouragement for this chapter is actionable and takes commitment, setting the time in your calendar, and implementing boundaries around you to ensure that you truly take this time to yourself. This is your time to dedicate yourself to rebuilding your foundation and building it strong & stable so that you can feel the safety in your body.

Breathing:
Have you ever watched a baby breathe?
Did you notice that they breathe from the belly?

Watching their little belly inflate and deflate with each inhale and exhale. As adults we begin to breathe with the chest, losing the belly breath...this is because we hold weight in the chest that we're trying to relieve, stress, and many years of unprocessed grief. Breathing from the belly allows more oxygen and blood to flow through the body because the abdomen is where all the blood vessels come to meet. When you're breathing with the belly, and giving more oxygen to the body, you can relieve stress, anxiety, etc., and breathe stronger.

Here's how you do this: Observe.

Observe your breathing naturally, is it shallow, slow, quick, deep, or short...what does it do?

Are your shoulders rising and falling? Is your belly moving? How do you feel?

Sit in stillness, close your eyes, and just observe yourself in your natural movement.

Now feel your breath – place your hand on your belly and another on your heart. Feel the 2 interact with one another. Notice the pace of your heart.

As you breathe, take a deep inhale to inflate your belly like a balloon.

On your exhale, let it all out from your mouth with a sigh or gentle exhale.

Repeat this 5-10x

Following this remove your hands and just observe your natural breathing, notice how you're feeling, notice the physical sensations and any emotions that arise or fall away.

This is one step to make space to breathe. Make space to grieve.

Mantra to repeat:
I am making space to breathe
I am safe
I will keep you safe
I will honor your needs
I am safe

I am safe
I am safe

Suggestion:
Do the breathing 3-5x per day or more ... at least:
1x when waking up before you begin your day
1x in the middle of the day
>1x before bed If you're able to find more time, take it!

Build the habit and build the strength of the breath, allow your lungs the space to process and release.

Make space for grieving and emotional release a 3-5x per week or as needed that feels good for you. You have grief set in from your own experiences from the time of you growing in your mother's belly, throughout this lifetime, past lifetimes and ancestors. It sounds like a lot, because it it! This is a practice that I've personally been doing for almost 10 years. I take time daily to process emotions, that could look like crying, dancing, walking, yoga, screaming or hitting a pillow, laughing, somatic movements...your options are endless. The more you make this a practice the better you will feel moving forward and the more you will reprogram your body to move out of the emotionally abusive cycle.

As you reprogram your mind and body, you will more easily identify these patterns as they arise in future months and years, the work has been done and you will have an easier time stepping away and not getting into these patterns anymore.

JOURNALING & MOVEMENT

Begin Your Morning:
What are you most grateful for each day?
Try to make time for this every morning, list 3 things per day you're grateful for. The action of gratitude helps you to find acceptance in where you are right here in the now and assists you to become more present.

Throughout Your Week:
Choose a movement that feels good for you, one where you move...walk silently, do yoga, dance, swim, hike, etc. And do this 3x per week...if not more often. Allow this time of movement to be present, connect to yourself, and let yourself be in the flow of what you're moving through.

After about a few weeks of getting some intentional movement in nature...when you return do the following journal and self-reflective exercise:

- How can you make more space for yourself to grieve?
- Can you set aside time to cry and break down, a time to go sit in nature, or take a long walk to move the body?

- How can you be more gentle with yourself as your emotions will ebb and flow?
- How can you find a deeper acceptance of what you're going through?
- How can you ask for help if you need it?
- Who is this person that you can reach out to when times and emotions are strained?

Connecting Deeper Through Boundaries

Developing a deeper connection to myself is something that took me years and am still in the process of creating that stronger connection, as I learn to ebb and flow with life. Like many things when I began my work, I didn't know that at the time I was committing to a new lifestyle pattern, not just making a change in that moment in time. A change where I would deeply go against the grain of my environment by consistently and repeatedly putting myself first.

Following the moment during my wedding preparations, of being asked how I wanted my wedding set up, and not knowing at all what I wanted, I felt as though something was profoundly missing. When I couldn't answer the one question that I assumed thousands of brides just KNOW right off the bat, this indicated to me that I'd somewhere, somehow misunderstood the assignment. The story I told myself was that I was the only bride or divorcee who didn't know what she wanted...and that made me feel small and embarrassed, to say the least.

Though this assumption got me onto the right track of gaining clarity, developing trust, and a love for myself many years later, I was wrong in my assumption that I was the only one who didn't know something that others did. Many of us don't know what we want or how to go after it. Perhaps more brides know this on the day of their wedding because they'd spent time and years thinking of it before the man ever came into the picture. This wasn't me, my only desire and knowing for my wedding was I wanted to be barefoot on the beach. That wasn't my wedding experience so other than that, I had no idea. This one contributing factor allowed me to see that not only did I not know my own wedding desires, but I also didn't know many of my life desires, I'd become so much like my ex-husband in his interests, likes, and dislikes, that I wasn't even sure what my own were.

After my divorce, when I first moved out and on my own, I felt like Julia Roberts in Runaway Bride, I literally tried all the egg styles and then some to discover how I liked my eggs. My commitment to myself to get to know myself better, began while I was still married and only deepened as the years went on following my divorce.

Following the wedding, I started noticing something bubbling up inside me that within a few short months, I was making it very clear to my ex-husband, that I wanted to travel. I didn't want to live in the city anymore, I wanted to live in a tiny house somewhere in the woods or near a beach, or perhaps both. I mentioned it to him over and over, every time he'd get stressed about life, money, or the giant home we lived in, I'd throw it right in the middle.

"Fuck it!" I'd say, "Let's sell the house, get a tiny house, hitch it to a truck, and live the van life traveling the country." He'd tell me how stupid and impractical that was and that he wanted no part of that lifestyle, he traveled too much for work and wanted to be at home and ground while he was off work. This made sense to me so I didn't argue it too much, though the desire to share went away less and less, it came up for me all of the time. I began seeing that this was an incompatibility within us that was a big one and I started wondering if it was one that would cause a divorce. How could we live together and be married if we both wanted different things out of life? This wondering led me to begin looking at him differently and myself differently. This is when I started noticing the abusive behavior and when he ultimately asked for a divorce early on in the marriage.

Just by me acknowledging this one deep incompatibility it enabled me to take off the designer rose-colored glasses that I'd been forcing myself to wear for years, and I didn't like what I saw. After he moved out I bought a book that was a workbook to help me through the beginning stages of getting to know myself and accepting pieces of myself that I'd unknowingly kept hidden. I got to a point where I could no longer hide the fact that I didn't want to be in the city, that I wanted to live abroad and I wanted to live a much more simple life than the one I'd been raised in. I had to admit that I wouldn't be satisfied in my life or ever truly happy if I remained in this abusive relationship, living in a city I never liked, wearing clothes that didn't suit me, and wearing shoes for God's sake! The amount of times I was in trouble with employers, before becoming self-employed, because I continuously was showing up to work without shoes on is high. I had a whole collection of shoes either lingering around in my tuck or I was sent to the local Target for a pair of cheap flip-flops to get me through the day. I was forcing myself to stay in a lifestyle that wasn't for me for the sake of the fact that it's what everyone around me was doing, only my misery had boiled over and the smoke alarm was going off. It was time to open the windows and step out for some fresh air to get to know the new me.

This wasn't an easy task, for me the programming that I'd been subjected to was heavy and woven deep into the fabric of my lineage, friends, and politics. I was submerged up to my eyeballs in a culture of programming that as I began to slowly step back, zoom out, and see the bigger picture, wasn't only suffocating myself but everyone involved. I didn't know many people who were truly on a deep level happy in their life and that made me sad, sad for me and sad for them, sad for the society that promoted and supported keeping the self-trapped in a story that denies one from getting to know themselves and finding acceptance in this space.

And sometimes we aren't even aware that this has become the case in our life until we get into a scenario such as in a relationship with a narcissistic or controlling personality type. This reveals how much you have allowed the world around you to control your likes, dislikes, and thought processes. This is how we maintain the status quo as a society, by allowing ourselves to be deeply influenced by the world around us, rather than choosing to be greater than our environment and stepping out to get to know the individual that we are. The relationship that you have with yourself will be and is the one and only most important relationship that you have, it's the most long-lasting and can be the most loving.

In the wake of allowing ourselves to be influenced by others this is when we abandon the self, deny the intuition, sacrifice our needs, put others before ourselves, play the martyr or victim, try to control those around us for our own comfort, and can become manipulative in order to get our way because we've lost sight so long ago. All of this dissipates as you develop a relationship with yourself when it's rooted in honesty and love.

All of this began with me developing boundaries and learning to be gentle with myself through the changes and through the opening of my eyes to myself and that around me.

BOUNDARIES

Probably the most powerful tool that I have learned is how to have, how to implement, and how to identify others...boundaries.

In order to have a healthy relationship with yourself or anyone else, you need to have healthy boundaries. Your boundaries derive from a place of being able to feel your feelings and know your likes and dislikes, you develop deeper boundaries the more you slow down and the less you distract yourself.

You have incoming and outgoing boundaries, you're setting the stage for how you will tolerate people treating you and how you will treat others. Sometimes you even need to set boundaries for people who don't know how to set boundaries for themselves, you can see they're letting everyone have a piece of their time, in which case, you have the self-awareness to know when it's time to set the boundary.

When you're in a relationship with a narcissist or raised by one, there's no room for boundaries. If boundaries are put into place it usually results in arguments and accusations, such things as, "You don't love me" or "You don't trust me" or the ever classic, "I'm not the one with the problem, it's you".

I'll never forget the first time I implemented a boundary, one that was light and said lightheartedly to my ex-husband, he looked at me with shock and while sitting with his family at the dinner table, he leaned over to say, "I think you need to stop going to therapy, it's making you assertive and I don't like you being assertive. You're not going to tell me what you're going to do." I leaned back, looked at him, and started laughing. Even now I laugh at this story, the audacity that he had to say this to me, in front of his family and show all his colors spoke volumes to me. My response was my way to cope and also to just tell myself, this logic isn't logic, it's fucked up and you've done nothing wrong.

Narcissists and people who are under the spell of a narcissist do not like boundaries, they are the ones who are meant to control the situation, not the other way around. They see boundaries as control, manipulation, projection, and bossiness, all because they are incapable of taking any responsibility for themselves, their word, or their actions. So even people who aren't narcissistic but have a need to control the situation won't like boundaries because they won't have a say in the situation and it will trigger their insecurities or fears. This is not your problem, I encourage you not to take this on as something else to manage.

Boundaries are, however, an act of love. For example: when you have a toddler who's learning the ways of the world, they reach a stage when they touch everything! They are developing their sensory responses, so everything gets picked up, touched, or put in the mouth. During this period you can allow them as much space as possible to explore while setting boundaries so they understand what's okay and not okay. When you set the boundary, it's for their safety, it's for their ability to not get hurt but they do what, they protest! Toddlers do not like boundaries, they want to be involved in everything. So what do you do? Do you let them walk to the edge of the stairs and let them figure it out? Do you open the front door and say, "Best of luck in your self-exploration"? No! You come up with words, actions, and sounds, that notify them they're reaching the boundary and it's not safe or not in their best interest to keep going that way. Over time, they learn that going to the edge of the stairs requires care, intention, and safety. They understand they need permission to go outside...etc.

Despite this analogy, when you begin to set boundaries after many years of "Leaving the front door open for anything to happen on your watch", then at first, it feels really gross. You get anxious, you feel the need to prepare yourself for the conversation, you worry if they'll get mad, and you aren't sure how to manage it if it goes past the words that come out of your mouth.

Setting boundaries is scary at first but is something that with practice comes more easily and it can truly deepen the relationship that you have with yourself. Personally, I found it easier to set boundaries with myself first and follow through...I did this for many years and slowly by doing this it would flow out with other people more naturally. It can help when setting new boundaries with yourself or another to en-vision setting boundaries with your toddler self. Be gentle and take care with your actions and words because you want to encourage self-exploration within yourself, while also creating a safe space to do so.

In order to set healthy boundaries you have to be able to recognize where your boundaries are being crossed and where they need to be strengthened. Again beginning with yourself is the easiest place to start and the best place to start because this is a huge part of deepening the relationship with yourself. Setting boundaries and following through builds so much from this one act! Self-trust, self-love, self-worth, confidence, and happiness grow when you set those boundaries over and over, and then follow through.

I quickly discovered when I set boundaries with those around me that it was often met with pushback, hurt feelings, or arguments. Sometimes this would become too much and I wouldn't set boundaries, intentionally setting myself up for discomfort in order to keep the peace because I was too tired to argue or defend myself, I just needed something to be smoother. While this may have worked in that moment, it didn't work in the long run and was overall not the best approach for any situation. This is a really common response when setting boundaries and being met with resistance or the need to defend yourself, you just get tired of the process and go through phases of not wanting to try. This doesn't help though, it doesn't help you to develop and it doesn't help those around you to develop within themselves.

This is why it's important to be aware of your feelings at all times. If you're feeling depleted, overwhelmed or overworked, raw and sensitive... and you anticipate boundary setting being a challenge with another individual, then this is potentially a great time for you to have some more time to yourself. Get recharged to feel stronger, more confident, and better about the boundary that needs to be set, you can put it off for just a short while to come back stronger. For this you'll need to be okay with communication and small boundaries, saying things like, "I have a lot on my plate right now, I'll reach back out to you next week." Or "Sorry, this doesn't work for me right now but I can reach out to you when it does." This communicates your needs in a small way and gives you a buffer space to regroup your nervous system in order to set that bigger boundary.

Once I became self-aware of this fact, that my trying to play peacekeeper didn't help I also learned there needs to be the energy to implement boundaries with yourself and others. When you are clearing deeper karmic patterns it can run down your energy levels, causing you to not always have the gumption to be firm with those around you, this is normal and totally understandable. Other times you might be easily triggered and quick to put up boundaries when they might not be needed as firmly or quickly as they went up, this is also very normal and understandable. There's always a balance with boundaries like everything else in life, you want to find that sweet spot and then do your best to let that sweet spot become part of your way of being.

When I first got divorced, I put up firm boundaries with almost everyone I know in every manner I could possibly think of. I was so hurt, so triggered, and so on edge in my nervous system that everything was a perceived threat. My nervous system was in fight & flight mode, doing its best to protect me. It ended up in some aspects of my life that I built walls around my heart with my boundaries to keep anyone from getting in to hurt me again. When the relationship that I'd had after my divorce ended, the walls got thicker and higher for several years. I didn't want to feel any of this pain ever again, anyone in my field could basically get fucked if they wanted something on a more serious level or even a deeper friendship. This benefited me at the time, and for a short while because I needed to know that I could protect myself, be there for myself, and stand in the gap when I needed it.

Then over time, the walls weren't needed and brick by brick, I dismantled them to slowly begin welcoming more love from friends, strangers, and myself. This is when I noticed that the walls had been up and were ready to fall away, it was hard, scary, and painful. It all began to slip away during my yoga teacher training in Bali, almost 3 years to the day following my divorce. The karma that was healing from my body was triggering everything within me. So much was happening at once, so many aspects and pieces of me were shedding that I was a total ball bag some days, crying over everything or nothing at all.

I remember sitting on the floor of the yoga shala in Ubud,

Bali, surrounded by rice paddies. I had begun noticing a pattern in the birds, about two minutes before a large storm the birds would leave the trees and fly in circles high above the tree line then nestle back into the trees together...and then the rains would fall. Buckets of water leaving the sky, sometimes you'd be yelling at one another because it was so loud as it beat against the tin roof of the shala. For some reason these storms would cause me to shake with anxiety, and uncontrollably cry, I didn't understand this response, it was involuntary and never happened to me before. I had to use my boundaries so much during yoga teacher training because I was surrounded by 30 people who constantly wanted to hug and I wanted no part of the hugging...so one afternoon during one of these rain storms, I sat on the floor crying, my fellow yogis respecting the "No hugging" boundary I'd put into place, all sat around me, up against my whole body, without hugging me or using their arms just used their body weight and love to surround me in genuine compassion.

This was my first taste of a group of women and people who were not offended by my boundaries, who wanted to respect them, and who also wanted me to know I was loved and supported. They did this several times, without a word, just walked over, sat down, leaned against me, and went about their own conversations or sat in silence while I cried. They knew that while I was strong and used to supporting myself, I was in uncharted territory and I didn't need to do it alone anymore. They respected the boundary I'd put into place because though we had only just met, they loved me and encouraged boundaries and open communication.

This boundary that I'd set was keeping love out, it was an unhealthy boundary over time, set in place to protect me, and wound up leaving me in isolation more often than not. I was afraid of love, afraid of letting anyone get close to me and to get hurt again. This wasn't helping me to gain a sense of sovereignty with myself, it was keeping me afraid. Their love and compassion allowed the boundary to melt into a more healthy boundary, for me to see that some people I want to hug and some people I don't, I don't need a reason and it doesn't have to be consistent. When we reference energy exchange, this makes sense, to have a healthy boundary and not hug anyone who has energy that you don't want. This is a whole other topic, but an example to understand the difference between healthy and unhealthy boundaries.

When you implement boundaries, it helps people to know how to love you, how to help, and how to be there for you. Boundaries open the line of communication for people to ask questions, get clear, and be direct without it needing to be personal. This is what will happen with the right people, people who are doing the work and who take the time to listen to you and give you the care you need. In turn, when you're ready to give back, you can be that for them as well.

These boundaries that are put into place during the healing phase of clearing karma are the most important, this is a time of you being very vulnerable, raw, and overall not yourself. When breaking out of a pattern you're letting go of a whole aspect of yourself and welcoming in a new one, having the courage to set boundaries allows you to move through your process at your own pace, not at the pace of what others expect. This is not their process so if people are offended by your boundaries it's because you're making them uncomfortable by healing, your actions for your life are causing them to look at themselves in a way that they don't want to. So if they push back and argue with you then it's usually a subconscious attempt on their psyche to protect themselves from themselves....allow yourself to not take it personally and stand firm in yourself.

The more you are able to stand fir" in 'our own boundaries the more you can build that trust within yourself, a trust so deep that your spirit knows that YOU GOT THIS! Trust is an important aspect of any relationship, especially the one you have with yourself. Over time this will build trust in others, the Universe, and the process of it all, assisting you to find joy in the journey.

With boundaries, trust, and communication, this deepens the relationship with yourself to feel confident to be able to clear the karmic pattern and break free of the cycle of emotionally abusive relationships or patterns. Without this, you end up living in fear or anxiety of others and therefore repeating the pattern because you're still in the vibration to attract more of it into your life. So even if you're not dating these types of personalities will come in the form of friends, co-workers, employees, etc. This is something that can take years to dissolve depending on how deep this wound goes for you.

For myself, it took years, the Universe over and over brought these types of personalities into my life. I had stopped dating these types of men but still, the friends I would make or someone within a work setting would gaslight or be verbally abusive towards me. Because I had only strengthened the boundaries I'd had with men, I still needed to work in these other areas, and over time, one by one I would release these friendships and open up for a more aligned friend who had their own boundaries and one their own deep work on this type of pattern.

Without boundaries in place with people you are sacrificing your needs and making yourself a martyr, this helps no one. You wind up overgiving and being the "Yes" person to where you get burnt out or resentment builds causing anger and you to be out of alignment. It's important when setting boundaries to take it slow, there's no rush and there's no need to push the situation. This gives you the space to be aware of your feelings, likes, and dislikes and act accordingly. If you're not present with your feelings and are in a rush then you'll end up saying yes when you mean no and putting the needs of others first, burning yourself out.

There are several ways to be able to identify if you have boundaries that need to be implemented or strengthened:

- You say Yes when you mean No
- You get pulled into situations that you otherwise wouldn't get involved in
- People call you to emotionally dump on you, not asking you if you have the space to listen or be present with them
- People call you to gossip, complain, or only when they have a problem
- You resent helping or giving to others
- You're burned out or overwhelmed with tasks

Here are a few ways to tell with whom you need to improve boundaries:

- If you say "No" and the other person argues or pushes back, maybe insists
- If you don't attend and someone gets mad at you
- If you disagree and another person becomes angry or argumentative
- If you tell someone they upset you, but they turn it around on you (this is also gaslighting)

It's important to recognize the difference between healthy and unhealthy boundaries. Many people set boundaries thinking they're healthy but when it's set to keep the world out, then it's unhealthy, it's blocking you from being connected to others. In the case of me not wanting hugs from anyone, this began because I have strong psychic abilities, when people hugged me, I would know what was going on or about to happen in their life. I didn't understand my gift or my ability to put up a healthy boundary with this so I just turned off all hugs, which didn't help me emotionally or physically.

Once I learned the value of protecting my energy and how to do this, I was able to hug people again without knowing all their business. I was then able to set an energetic boundary that was healthy to protect my energy from the outside world, by being present with how I felt. If I wanted to hug someone, I would, that wasn't crossing the boundary. If I didn't want to hug someone but did anyway, out of a sense of obligation, then that would be crossing my personal boundary because I did what I didn't want to do.

Boundaries take a long time to learn, understand, and simplify for yourself. Being patient and gentle with this process, and letting mistakes be made without shame are key to developing healthy boundaries with yourself.

If you're new to boundary setting, as mentioned it can feel pretty fucking gross and uncomfortable at first, but totally normal, be aware of it and take note of your response, over time it will get easier.

Here are a few ways to begin implementing boundaries:
If you catch yourself over-giving your time, then instead of accepting every invitation, try:

> "Let me check my calendar" or "I'll have to get back to you"

This allows you the space to check in with yourself to see if it's something you really want to do, or if you have the time, energy, and bandwidth for another "To Do" set in your calendar. If you don't have the time, then say so:

"I won't be able to attend, but I'd like to rain check with you."

Taking the word "No" back to toddler days, it connects to the inner child this way also, sometimes if we say this word to people who aren't doing boundary work it sets them off. When you rephrase it into something that's deemed less harsh, then you're able to connect better to the other person. So if your boss asks you to work late often, then this needs to be handled in a way to not piss off your boss right, using any of the above phrases works and gets your point effetely across.

If the word "No" is hard for you to say, then try:

"That's not going to work for me" or "I'm not available for that"

If you're invited to do something you used to do, but no longer want to participate in, for whatever reason, try this:

A friend invites you to the bar and you don't want to go to bars anymore...it's their birthday and you're expected but you know that this environment isn't the best for you. Obligation or guilt can arise, and while explaining isn't always needed, there are times when it helps.

"Thank you so much for inviting me, I'd love to celebrate

This lets your friend know where you stand and why, especially if a lifestyle pattern is changing and they're not used to it yet. The friend will either be in support and understand or they won't. I've had many friends attempt to pressure me into bar activities after I stopped going and drinking, so sometimes it was hard to stay firm. These friends ultimately stopped being my friends because we didn't have that one lifestyle in common, but that's okay with me because I honored myself. My honoring of myself was triggering for these friends because they themselves wanted to stop going to bars but couldn't break the pattern.

If you find yourself needing to set firmer boundaries with people who resist or argue with you when a gentle boundary is set, then I encourage you to be strong. If needed, ask a supportive friend to help you or a therapist for support. Our society is so un-used to boundaries that even the nicest people can resist boundaries sometimes out of fear of losing a friend, they take it personally or become offended. Their response isn't your responsibility. But there are firmer options for you to get your point across.

Such as:

"I've mentioned a few times that I won't be doing X, but you keep insisting. So I'm going to be making {this} change between

us because I no longer want to argue with you about this." And MAKE THE CHANGE

"If you shout at me, I will leave." And WALK AWAY

The follow-through in setting the boundary is the most important part. Few people will remember the words you spoke but they will remember the action. Some people can be so in denial of who they are or unable to hear you that these boundaries are necessary.

When you set a boundary be okay with some people exiting your life, let them go. Your boundaries are for you, not to be moved around for the comfort of others. Be prepared when you set a boundary to follow through...while also knowing you can change your mind. If you change your mind, then make sure it's for the right reasons, not because you're being pressured or feel obligated.

Personally, I have gently broken up with friends before who are unable to follow the boundaries that I've set. If someone keeps pushing past a boundary with me, I will usually say ONE TIME, that they're not listening to me, and inform them how that feels. Sometimes this helps, sometimes not...on the ones who it doesn't help with then I block them. One of the beauties of technology is the BLOCK BUTTON! When all else fails, the block button usually helps in light scenarios. Of course in extreme cases, like with my ex-boyfriend's Ex, filing a restraining order is another "Don't fuck with me" boundary, that sometimes needs to come into play. But for the average person verbal boundaries usually work, if they don't though, don't hesitate to go as far as you can for your peace.

Set the boundary, follow through, to build trust and safety in your body over and over again.

SLOW DOWN, BE GENTLE, BE PRESENT

So much goes into clearing these karmic patterns, so much time, energy, love, and waves of emotions to move through. Being present with your emotions helps you immensely as does adopting gentleness with yourself, not shaming or blaming yourself for anything.

Remember that you've come from a space where you weren't acknowledged by your partner(s), nor by yourself. So, you're now taking time to do this, to acknowledge yourself, and to play witness to all of the pain that's coming out, the grief that you're moving through, and the new changes to implement that it can be a challenge to stay connected to yourself.

Slowing down through this healing process is one of the greatest gifts I ever gave myself. To slow down and to really give me the space that I needed without the need to distract or look away from myself when I did the deeper work. This is always the first thing we want to do when the emotions are too much or the truth is too painful to see, we distract and try to rush through or bypass. I've done this so many times out of fear of myself or fear of my emotions. However, once I stopped that pattern and slowed down to just be present, I discovered that being present and being gentle with myself was far more rewarding than it was to bypass the situation.

Honestly, I didn't possess this until moving to Bali, it provided me the tools and lifestyle that I needed to fully lean into this. While I lived in the West, the lifestyle is fast-paced and promotes you to bypass many areas of your life that are simply "inconvenient". Once I slowed down, I was forced to set new boundaries and feel new feelings...and it was more than scary, it was petrifying.

Slowing down causes the mind and body to resist heavily. The ego mind wants you to be in constant productivity because this is how society has been set up, to be productive every waking moment. But this is so unsustainable, not to mention, it's physically, emotionally & spiritually unhealthy, causing all kinds of issues.

When I first slowed down to become more present, I had waves of emotions so intense that I began having panic attacks. This happened when I got a divorce when I began traveling alone through Asia, and again when I moved to Bali to live. During the previous years, I was self-medicating through these emotions using alcohol and caffeine, but when I moved to Bali I'd quit all of that. I was face to face with some pretty intense emotions, so intense that I reached out to my therapist who pointed out that it sounded like a hormone imbalance.

I contacted a Traditional Chinese Medicine practitioner who did a work over and turns out, yes, I was having major hormone imbalances, not to mention my nervous system had been in fight or flight for most of my life. I'd been having it for years only I hadn't slowed down long enough to hear my body tell me that it was needing help. Once I had some sessions of acupuncture, and some Chinese herbs, shifting a few things in my diet, within a few months I was back on track to feeling and doing great! I no longer had the scary waves of emotions that weren't me at all, but my body reacting to the imbalance of my nervous system.

When we're bypassing and not present with ourselves, we are missing major signs from the body that are saying it needs special attention. Often it's such an easy fix of herbs and food adjustment but gone untreated for years it develops into something much worse. This is how the West treats it...to ignore the problem, hope it will go away then rush to the doctor the minute things get worse. Then the doctor prescribes a little pill of sorts, sometimes multiple because you can never have just one, and then the problem seems to go away. But it's really just a band-aid for the issue that's more deeply rooted, the emotions that need attention, the grief that needs to be released, and the lack of boundaries in one's life.

Learning to be present, and slow down helps you to create

that gentleness with yourself, and the strength to boundary set regularly. By being gentle with yourself you're more willing to sit with the emotions of the body and let them play out so that you can move into a new vibration. So that you can enjoy slowing down, enjoy being present without the running of thoughts all through your mind because you've slowed down to gently listen and give them the time of day.

When you slow down, you open up to have the willingness and courage to feel the feelings. It allows you to see the signs from the Universe to let you know when you're in alignment or out of alignment. It opens up the communication within yourself, to be honest, be present, be aware, and be available for yourself. This takes your relationship with yourself to a whole new level because you're making time to see yourself and acknowledge your needs in a gentle, non-judgmental way.

This is a huge act of self-love! You don't have to go very far in your memory bank to see times within this narcissistic or emotionally abusive relationship pattern when you weren't seen or needs weren't acknowledged, slowing down to see yourself now speaks volumes to the relationship you have with yourself. It builds a deeper level of trust and strengthens the communication to be so on point that your boundaries ebb and flow beautifully without the need to worry or sacrifice the self to get your needs met, you're already doing it!

***

BOUNDARIES OBSERVATION & JOURNALING

This exercise is best done with the dedication of a few hours over the course of a week.
- Go slow when setting boundaries
- Be aware
- "Stalk yourself"

Take note of your current boundaries in one area of your life, choose one person or one scenario to examine, and be particular and open to the critique.

Without any changes watch this situation as it plays out over a week or two, then get to work with identifying and slowly shifting the boundaries.

This is one that will take time especially if there are no current boundaries in place, if you're close with a person you can even tell them you're doing boundaries work and see their response. They may get curious and it could be a great opportunity for both of you to grow together with better boundaries. If they don't get curious or push the conversation aside quickly, this is your sign that they aren't ready for this type of work with you. Don't force or take it personally. This is all for you, you cannot force another person to join your work.

SELF-REFLECTIVE QUESTIONS:

- How are your boundaries in this scenario, are you happy with them?
- Do they feel healthy or unhealthy?
- Do you like how the boundary is in place or dislike it?
- What are your feelings surrounding this particular scenario?
- What if anything, needs to be shifted? Are you willing to shift the boundary?
- Will shifting the boundary to a healthier space cause any resistance to you or another person?
- How can you best support yourself through the shift of boundaries?
- How can you use this as an example for other areas of your life?

SLOWING DOWN:

- Where in your life can you slow down to be more present and less distracted?
- What boundary needs to be set in order to achieve this?
- In what way do you need to listen to the needs of your body better?

- How much would slowing down affect your life-style?
- What are the best-case scenario "What ifs"?
- How can you best support yourself by slowing down and being more present?

7

From Surviving to Thriving

It's amazing how we can CHOOSE to see life a certain way versus another. It's all in the perspective that's chosen, the stories we hold, our experiences, or how we're programmed... this shapes all of our choices and responses to how we show up in life.

For many years, I chose to look at myself and my circumstances as a victim...not seeing how much I had been through and overcome...only choosing to see what was taken away, the shame and the pain that it brought. I was going through life for many years following my divorce in what my mom called "Relationship PTSD". I was easily triggered by those around me when it would hit at those core wounds that I hadn't yet taken the time to understand and work toward healing.

I carried with me the messages and vibration that I "wasn't going to make it", which were words said to me by several narcissistic people throughout my life. I held on to this message of unworthiness for so many years, letting it seep into every corner of my being and tainting my perspective of myself. I chose to hold on to this, it was a story few people learned about me, until you read this right now, and it was something that I felt if I let go of, who would I be?

Who would I be if I wasn't the woman holding this wound in her back pocket? All the while, traveling the world, having 2 successful businesses, and making loads of friends. Manifesting wonderful men out of the woodwork over and over who may not have been in long-term relationships but were all kind individuals showing me that I was worthy of being loved. Who would I be if this story didn't propel me forward, out of fear? The fear of not making it.

I had allowed this story to in a way cripple me, stunt my spiritual and emotional growth so profoundly that I would get so bent out of shape when the wound was touched. I would become enraged at myself and at the Universe for letting me live this story out, saddened that it was something that affected me so deeply, yet wouldn't leave. While living in Bali, is when several friends gently said to me, "You're playing the victim and it's no longer serving you." I knew that I needed to make some sort of change within myself if I ever wanted my perspective to shift, if I wanted to grow, and if I wanted to call in a whole new lifestyle.

I needed to find my voice and stand in the gap for myself. It occurred to me that those around me in the "past life" that I shared with my ex-husband, were manipulating and controlling my moves, my decisions, and my life for their own comfort. And the worst part...I had allowed this behavior in my life for many years. Even long after they physically were out of my life, their words and energy were still controlling how I showed up in my life! What the hell is that? This was evident to me that the DNA in my body was carrying these stories despite my spirit and mind doing their best to rewrite the narrative.

The time had come when I needed to take serious responsibility for myself, my actions, and my words. By continuing to stay in the victim mindset, I was self-sabotaging my life that was trying to be created. I felt like I was a walking contradiction. On one hand, I was saying that I was strong, independent, happy, and creating the type of life I wanted; all while on the other hand, I wasn't showing up as this person, I didn't believe in myself or my abilities, I was living in fear of being alone, and I wasn't happy with where I was in life.

I needed to take a step back, zoom out, and look at the bigger picture that is me and that is the woman that I was longing to be. I needed to step out of a victim mentality and into a thriving mentality, even if things weren't looking the way I wanted them to look. I was allowing myself to show up and vibrate as a victim, so naturally the Universe continued to bring me people and situations that supported this belief system that I was living out.

I won't sit here to place blame on anyone in my life then or now, we each have a responsibility to our own actions of what we are putting out into the world and what we are receiving from the world. As I look back then and even in my life some- times now, I allow myself to be taken advantage of when I'm just overall exhausted, when I don't have much energy to give, and when I do my best to give to myself.

When I'm in these lower vibrational places, I notice it becomes easier for me to get taken advantage of, not even by malicious people, just people also tired and not wanting to do the work. The story that I'm carrying is calling that into my field, so it's important to take note of the healing journey of your vibration and the energy that you're broadcasting out there, by the stories that you're holding and releasing.

Sometimes we are low and that's our best, and that's okay...these are times to keep more to yourself, have more sol- itude, say 'No' more often, and give a little bit of extra energy to yourself. Be okay with being alone, and keeping yourself company, it's all worth it when your vibration comes back up!

That being said, I've taken into deep consideration that through various points in my life thus far I have been manip- ulated or emotionally blackmailed in some way by those around me. As I worked through my healing journey, I could see that those people were themselves being manipulated or controlled by another force in their lives. It was a vicious cycle that most of us are completely oblivious to...the spirit knew full well and the lifestyles reflect this inner discomfort. Yet without being consciously aware, both parties (myself &

another) were perpetually circulating in a cycle of manipulation in order to get our needs met. It took me being willing to stand in front of a mirror, to acknowledge the part that I was playing, and make the choice for myself to learn a different pattern of relating to people. Therefore, I learned to meet my own needs rather than be in a cycle of manipulation or control to get those needs met by others.

While I was in these types of emotionally abusive relationships, the narcissism was projected out and through the lens of extreme insecurity; a low sense of self-worth; lack of selflove; unhealed pain, and trauma. I can see it in my own actions from that period of my life...I would take it on, then through my own insecurities and unhealed wounds, would project in some way manipulative, controlling, fearful traits. This is a part of the cycle when people are operating in life through their wounds and insecurities, hiding in shame rather than healing themselves.

As a Highly Sensitive Person and Intuitive (though I didn't know it then), when I took on and projected this pain, it would physically hurt my body. This is why I was so sick my whole life!! I was affected by those around me, the energy that was held unknowingly by myself and by my environment had made me sick. Since I was going through painstaking efforts to separate myself from these patterns, I was still getting sick and playing witness to the Victim Mindset of how much it was controlling my life, my health, and my mental well-being...because it was my vibration.

This is what I did, took a step way, way back, to be in deep solitude unlike any other time before and begin to observe myself and my current way of being. To observe how I was showing up in the world versus how I wanted to show up in the world...My goal with this was to get to know myself outside of the programming, outside of the self-sabotage, and outside of the way that I'd been showing up. I wanted to choose to be happy and I wanted something I could be happy about because how I was showing up was making me unhappy. There are no two ways to look at it, I was going through the motions of life while not feeling true happiness and contentment with who I was.

I was a woman who'd traveled and lived all over the world. I was a woman who'd sold everything she'd owned to move to the other side of the world to follow an unknown calling and a need to be in Bali, only to be in such deep solitude. Yet the lifestyle that I had been in and was in wasn't satisfying and my health was still in decline...so I needed to shift and shift dramatically.

It took me a long time to learn and understand that the Universe mirrors back to me all that I'm feeling or thinking. I needed to learn that I have the power to create my own reality. That all my fears, insecurities, and self-sabotage behavior would be mirrored back to me through those around me.

Same thing for a narcissistic relationship, the narcissist

mirrors back to you all your insecurities. They are master manipulators because they can energetically sense what I or you are broadcasting and mirror back, through the form of emotional or verbal abuse. Narcissists are good at poking these insecurities and fears, then walking away not caring at all while you crumble.

when I learned that my insecurities and deeply rooted self-sabotage behavior were being mirrored back; I had two options, take it as an opportunity to heal myself and thrive. Or absorb it and live inside the stories, allowing them to pull me deeper into the emotionally abusive behavior.

Throughout the years of healing, I've ebbed and flowed through these states of being. I would be thriving for many months, rewriting stories in my head, reprogramming my DNA, and healing. Then through a trigger moment, I'd be right back in the bottom of the hole I'd dug without any desire to get out, the fear would outweigh me. After some time at the bottom, I'd get sick of the shit and climb out or snap out to begin another deeper layer of healing.

I'm so grateful to this lesson of awareness over the years because it's something that during my low times in the past, I'd be overly hard on myself rather than recognize that this was part of the pattern. We can only heal as deep as we're willing to go and willing to see, we each reach points in the healing journey over and over where we aren't ready or willing to see a pattern. When we're ready to see it is when it's revealed so that it can be shifted. I learned to appreciate the highs and the lows because without one you cannot have the other, each is there to teach you and propel you forward.

SHIFTING OUT OF MY WOUNDED SELF

As I was in this state, I was observing and learning about myself and the wounds I carried on a whole new level. I learned something powerful, when you're under long-term stress of narcissistic abuse it alters the way that your brain functions, causing long-term PTSD (PostTraumatic Stress Disorder). The way in which you view the world or those around you is altered to a level that prevents you from connecting to others more deeply out of fear. Or because you're hyper-vigilant to watch their every move and word, over-analyzing their behavior to see if they too are going to become emotionally abusive. Once I learned this, just before sitting down to write this book, I sat back again to examine my current and past relationships since my divorce, to play witness to the fact that for almost eight years I'd been in this state of hyper-vigilance with every man I dated and every friend I made, male or female.

Knowing this to be an unfair perspective to place on my friends and myself, I did what I do best, I got out of my head and into my body. I noticed how I physically felt around people rather than what my head, fear, or stories were trying to tell me. As soon as I did this, I was able to truly connect more deeply to all my friends, I have reconnected with some and stayed disconnected with others. I forgave myself for not knowing this sooner and released the need to be in this state of arousal so that my connection to myself could grow deeper and I could truly leave behind this state of victimhood.

I needed to identify that my wounded self was being governed by my fear of being abandoned, through this fear I would do my best to control the world around me. To control things so that they arrived or left on my terms and nothing else, in the wake of this I would push people away from me or I would cling to them tightly so that I didn't have to make a change. I never thought of myself being one to not want to change, but there were for sure aspects of my life that I was totally unwilling to change. Through this fear I kept many and most people at an arm's length distance from me, literally, I would barely let people hug me. One reason why I did this so that I could observe them and be prepared if it seemed like they were going to leave me in some way, I'd see it coming. And then I could leave first, telling myself this process would hurt less. I believe this story to be one that I needed to hold for a little while after my divorce but quickly recognized that I'd held it too long and it was now hindering me from growing.

This I know was caused by the fact that I didn't see my divorce coming, I didn't see that he would ever leave. I knew we had problems and I knew I was unhappy, but I didn't see the finale coming at all, I didn't want to. So in the wake of this trauma, I was doing my best attempt to always see it coming. I was trying to avoid feeling shame or having the rug pulled out from me and so in this fear, I missed some great moments or opportunities with people. I kept such control of the situation that even when there were men who wanted something longer term with me, I'd be quick to push it away or not let things develop deeper in order to avoid getting hurt.

People can sense this, whether they realize it or not. The spirit is always in tune, even when the mind and body are going in other directions, as is the case with many of us living through the lens of our trauma.

During my time of solitude and taking a step back, I was able to observe these behaviors without judgment or placing blame on myself for anything. I was able to see myself and say, "Oh you're not failing at relationships, you just don't want one yet and that's totally okay. You don't feel safe in one, so if you want one, how can you learn to feel safe in another relationship again? How can you move out of playing the victim and into thriving in your life?"

This is the power of being in a space of solitude to heal the mind and body, is to be able to play witness to the self to see how you're showing up in life through a non-judgmental lens and instead being more loving, gentler, and more accepting.

Leaving a narcissistic relationship and getting a divorce did dramatically change me, and how could it not? I developed or deepened an abandonment wound, I didn't and sometimes don't trust people, and I unknowingly developed a suspicious air about myself. These types of radical lifestyle changes are times in your life where there's very clearly a Before and an After, where you were one person then you go into a Dark Night of the Soul to emerge a totally different person. This is normal, it takes time and it takes patience that some days or many days you just want to throw in the towel and scream out, "WHAT'S THE POINT?"

As I have moved through this healing journey, the amount of times I've said this in moments of desperation and confusion could have made me rich, if someone paid me each time. You are actually re-wiring the brain and how it operates after being literally damaged through this form of abuse. It takes time for the body to break itself down and then rebuild itself back up. We want to know why we're experiencing something or why it feels like it's not working out...when in reality the point is that it's a process, unlearning your unworthiness and learning to fall in love with yourself cannot be rushed.

Without getting too much into the science of it, the long-term effect of narcissism on the brain causes to you react and live more from your "Lizard brain", or the Amygdala, which is in charge of the fight or flight response, fear, sexual drive, and other emotional responses. When you're living from this space then you're having more fearful responses to life, more emotional reactions to later look back and say, "That's not how I feel" despite the action being the opposite of the internal calm state emotion. Your nervous system is a total wreck in fight or flight mode, and unsure how to actually respond so its erraticism causes all types of imbalances in the body.

The Amygdala also controls the heart rate and breathing, which when damaged causes panic attacks and other shortness of breath issues. When this area is damaged by narcissistic abuse and you are healing from the abusive patterns, your body has physical responses that are scary and uncontrollable. You're learning how to control your body again rather than allowing it to remain in these fight or flight responses and not letting it continue to deteriorate over time.

When children are in these environments with a narcissist, the damage to their little bodies reacts in similar ways and can sometimes be irreversible without extra attention, care, and therapy for many years. As they will need to work to reshape the parts of the brain that have been damaged. This is when narcissism as a trait is learned in childhood, many psychologists say that narcissism is hard to reverse in adults because it has totally changed the wiring of the mind.

After learning this and watching my own patterns, I give myself and others from narcissistic abuse a huge amount of grace. Doing this healing work takes time and care that sometimes feels too much to bear, without an end in sight. I know that any little effort and accomplishment, while seemingly small to some is a huge weight off and a major accomplishment to the one doing the healing work. Every step toward healthiness is a step in the right direction.

In terms of having friendships with others also healing

from this type of abuse, over the years I have developed a boundary with people who have been raised by a narcissist in addition to being in a relationship with them, to have these friends not as close to me as someone without this experience. I never understood why my intuition told me to do this but after learning about the effect on the brain, it makes sense.

As much as we don't want to admit it, we can pick up the behavior of those people that we're around, they say that you exhibit the behavior or thought processes of the 5 closest people to you. If one of them has or is a narcissistic person then you do pick up these behaviors even when you're not a narcissist. You become a person who either develops these tendencies or becomes like me, emotionally detached through the trauma.

This is a healing that takes years and is intentional. When friendships are formed with the intent to support one another who has been in this type of scenario before, but who actually bond over the trauma, then over time, the friendship ends up doing more harm than good for each other. Not because these friends don't care but because each person is on their own healing journey from this abuse and will end up every time exhibiting the behavior of a narcissist without even realizing it. Some do not want to admit it through shame that they could have these behaviors, so the amount of friends in this healing realm that I've broken up with is too many to count. Not because I didn't care for them, but ultimately because they began being abusive or very manipulative towards me and I wasn't going to tolerate it anymore. When I called them on their behavior, giving them a chance to make the change, the weight was so shameful that they'd just deny it and gaslight me instead. So I'd end the friendship, and grieve yet another friendship, praying it would open me up for a friend who wasn't also healing from narcissistic abuse.

At this time of my life, the 5 closest people to me have not had any narcissistic abuse and therefore I have been able to heal on a deeper level. These boundaries can be hard to put into place with those you love but are very necessary to your healing process. By finding the courage to implement these boundaries, and remove myself from the environment causing the repeat patterns, I have been able to see a broader way to love one another and find a different type of support.

This has allowed me the ability to see that I can be loved and supported without shame or manipulation ever coming into play within the friendship. I've found people who can communicate honestly with themselves and bear little shame to be able to say who they are with others. When you're only in the narcissistic environments, this is how you know how to love, this is all you've ever been shown. So if and when you want to break those patterns for yourself then you have to find new surroundings of some kind. It doesn't mean you have to go "no contact" with people who are also healing from narcissistic abuse but it means the boundaries in place need to support your growth and no one else.

Traveling and moving away from my environment was the best thing I did for myself, I realize this isn't available for everyone. So in this case it boils down to, what can you shift within your environment to help yourself see a new perspective? Do you need to limit time with certain friends or family members, in order to branch out in other ways to try new things, have new experiences, and meet new people?

This was the most powerful part of my traveling to Bali was meeting new people from all over the world. When I was still living in Texas I would take short weekend trips all over Texas or to other states to do new things. I'd join dance classes, singles groups, workshops, art projects, volunteering, etc. to get out of my house, out of my comfort zone, and meet new people to have those new experiences. Sometimes this would get me right back into old patterns but with new people, this is because I hadn't yet dealt with the underlying issues that were causing these patterns to arise. So if this happens to you, then it's a clear sign some underlying issues need to be addressed before you can fully embark on something wildly new. Otherwise, you'll just take the old shit with you when you go and that never works, it'll always come back around for you to address it, always!

In order to leave the way of living within the wounded space, you first identify the wound, then say how you want to show up versus how you're showing up now in relation to that wound. When you've decided to show up outside of the wound, then every encounter becomes the opportunity to leave the wounded space little bit by little bit.

For example: I identified a wound of feeling unworthy of love and was pushing others away because of it, therefore assisting in the support of this belief. I then identified ways in which I could begin supporting myself to not only feel worthy of love from those around me but most importantly with myself.

DISCOVERING YOUR WORTHINESS

Discovering your worthiness is a tricky part of the healing and recovery process to overcoming emotional abuse of any kind. This is something that's taken me years because it has so many layers and we each evolve in our own way and time frames.

It's a tricky piece to the puzzle and here's why, unveiling your worthiness to come to a true inner knowing that you're deserving of love and all the great things your heart desires is something that only you can give yourself, no one else, nothing else.

The tricky part is that at the beginning of the recovery journey, you need the external validation of others. You need people in your corner who believe in you, who see you when you're at your lowest, who encourage you to keep going when times are hard, who call you on your shit, and who love you completely. These people are the ones who show you a new depth to yourself, and the power with which you hold. That's why those 5 people that you surround yourself with are vital to your healing process and the journey that you're embarking on. They don't need to be on the same or even similar journey but they need to have your back!

Having this experience and encouragement through their love and seeing yourself through their eyes, helps you in each step of the way to learn to more deeply love yourself. To get to a point where you have your back! Where you have that inner knowing that you fully trust in yourself, that you deserve all of your heart desires, that you don't self-sabotage your growth and effort, and that you continue to see yourself with unconditional love through your own eyes.

This is how you begin to find your worthiness and over time explore how you can deepen this connection to yourself. The trick is to allow these people into your heart just enough to give this gift to you while being mindful not to become codependent on them or rely on them for your happiness. I mention this because when coming out of emotionally abusive patterns, you're also healing from codependency and learning to be more dependent on your own, something that's new to the psyche and body.

One reason why I know it took me longer to get to this inner worthiness is that I would get hung up on the opinions and perspectives of others for too long, allowing those opinions to control how I viewed myself. I sometimes would get so caught up that their words would go against my intuition and I would cause myself so much confusion, grief, and heartache, trying to force myself to conform to the box with which they were putting me in. Rarely was this ever malintent of another but someone living inside their own stories of unworthiness, that were being projected onto me or triggered by my experience.

See, while these five people are amazing and vital for your healing journey, it's important to remember and witness them as humans, also having their own human experience. They will come to you with their own perspectives that were cultivated through their own experiences of women/men, friends, family, work, money, etc., and the world around them. They're words and actions towards you will nine times out of ten be in love, but will also be through their own lens. I learn to hear what they say but only take what you need and leave the rest. This phrase has become my life's motto in recent years, it's something my therapist always said to me, "Take what you need, and leave the rest."

This means accepting what's being said that resonates and works for you and for the pieces that don't work for you, let it go. Don't hang on to it, don't overthink it, don't feel guilty for not listening when someone gave you their thoughts, let it go. If someone gets upset that you don't take their advice, then know that's again their own story in their mind and has nothing to do with you. I have learned to thank people for their time and energy, and reply with, "I'm going to think about this and see how it applies to me". This shows my friend I value their time, which I do, and it gives me the space and permission to do what's best for me without added pressure from another.

Another saying that I heard once from a man I had a weekend fling with helps me to this day, many years later...he said, "Opinions are like assholes, everyone has got one, and they all stink. Don't let other people's opinions and stink affect you, you have your own asshole to worry about." A bit of a crass saying but nonetheless, I found it hysterical and it's something that's stuck! People really value their opinion of others' lives, they really think that they know what's right because what they're telling you is probably very right for them. Keep in mind the world is a mirror, they mirror for you, but you're also mirroring for them.

As soon as I truly began taking all of this to heart, in that time when I was in my solitude, it helped me tremendously. I had to see and acknowledge that I'd taken it to heart and was trying to force it to work, the opinions of others, including psychics, my therapist, and my best friends. While they all meant well and came to me in love, some of their words or opinions were hindering me from finding my own inner worthiness, because I was allowing it. Just another old pattern and habit of someone who's had a lot of narcissistic abuse, allowing others to govern my life.

Old habits are hard to break, and it took me over a year to break this one, which is why I share it with you today. Don't let the opinions of others dictate your life, use them instead as a soundboard for getting to know yourself and finding that inner voice and guidance that won't lead you astray. For that matter, don't even hang on to the words I've shared in this book, if something I say doesn't resonate with you, let it go, leave it. Only take with you what's resonating, what feels good, and what is helping you to find that deep love and worthiness for yourself. Because once you complete this book and put it down, some of my words will help you but many of them will go out the window to make space for something you desire or need to remember.

Using this concept with others will help you to find that balance in the healing journey. It will assist you to be able to build trust in yourself while also the ability to connect with those around you that are solid friends. Sometimes the words of a confidant can be seeds planted in the psyche. You may not be ready for them but in time they can come back in a moment when you're ready to follow through. And you'll be thankful to that person for the time they took to speak their truth.

Once I began to truly embody this and let go of the things others said that I was holding on to, I began to find the worthiness within myself that I had been looking for for so long. It's almost like it just miraculously appeared one day and I was like, "Oh shit, there you are!" It took some time to arrive and I needed to move through some deep wounds but ultimately it was there. The words of friends, and therapists, were the seeds they planted but I wasn't ready to hear it and wasn't able to understand it. When I say, "It's there", please know that like everything else, it's small at first but with nurturing and care has been growing daily over time. Causing me each day to be so grateful for my painful experiences to get to the point of deeper self-love and letting go of living in the wounded space.

One of the biggest wounds I moved through was believing in myself. I had gotten very hung up on the fact that people kept saying to me, "You just need to love yourself more". This had become a huge trigger phrase to me. If one more person said this, I would easily have snapped. In order to avoid this conversation, I stopped sharing what I was going through with people for a short while because I needed to understand what this meant for me, not what it meant for them or what they thought I should be doing.

Acknowledging that I didn't believe in myself to make it work was a hard pill to swallow. I needed to first identify where this story came from, my ex-husband and another member of my family as a child, told me, I'd never make it. I saw that I'd been carrying this story or what I now call a hex, around for most of my life and living out of fear of it, letting it propel me in fear rather than operating in love.

I wondered, "How can I let this go?" I first needed to

release that idea that I cared what others thought...that one was easy, was I really going to let two people who were long out of my life dictate what I thought of myself? Hell no! Then I needed to rebuild the story within me and give myself the evidence that not only was I going to make it, but that I had been making it all along. I just was choosing to not see it, because I was too busy with the fear of this other story.

I spent months making lists and writing in my journal my accomplishments, big or small, they all got recognition...I wrote about my two successful businesses that I closed in order to move to Bali or to pursue other dreams...I made it then. I wrote about my trips around the world, working and living in several countries...traveling on my own when everyone said it couldn't be done. I wrote about my finances and how well I'd lived on a budget, saved, invested, and was otherwise very successful there. I wrote about the men I'd dated and how beneficial each one was for my life, post leaving the emotionally abusive pattern of men. I wrote about my spiritual awakening and journey, how every year I'd developed a deeper relationship with myself, and that I'd made it to this point in my life to write a book, a lifelong dream.

After I'd written these pieces in my journal to prove to myself that I was not only doing it, but was going to make it even farther, and was making it in the present moment...all with the Universe supporting me every step of the way, I'd shift my energy somehow. I'd follow these journal exercises with a dance, sing, doing yoga, walk in the garden, get on my scooter, go to the beach, have a hike, etc. I'd do something that I loved to help me release the old story and embody the new one.

In the coming months, I was not only knowing that I was going to make it but I felt that deeper sense of worthiness that I was seeking. I was connecting more to myself and therefore more to Spirit and the Universe, who was so excited for this deeper transformation that gifts began coming in quickly. I was here to welcome it one right after the other as each one showed me how supported and worthy of love I was. I had reached a point after many years, that I knew I was worthy of being loved and I could still acknowledge how this was an emotional stretch for me into something new, but it felt better than remaining in the fear of never making it ever gave me.

This is the beauty in the balance, allowing others to show you a different way to love, then taking those pieces that work for you and showing this love for yourself. The underlying reason why many of us following a relationship with a narcissist feel unworthy is that who we are was beaten down, we were made to think we were crazy and gaslit when we tried to stand up for ourselves. That inner fire was slowly quenched and now it's up to you to rebuild it by showing yourself the love that you deserved but didn't and would never receive from this relationship.

It's a delicate step and again, like many things in the healing journey requires your best patience with yourself. As you begin to validate your feelings, your experiences, your opinions, and support yourself through this process while also welcoming in support from those beloved and trusted friends.

There are pieces of you that have been chipped away not only from this relationship but through other experiences in childhood or with friends that led you into this type of relationship. There are karmic patterns of unworthiness that have been running through your lineage and by you shifting it, it takes time. The time that you have to rebuild yourself into the version of the person you wish to show up as, the person whom you want to be around, relate with, and develop a deeper connection to. This isn't something that miraculously happens one day, you have to decide who you want to show up as and begin being that person.

For example; if you want to be a person who homesteads but lives in the city, then begin an herb garden, spend more time in nature, get involved in a community garden...do something that resonates with you as a homesteader and start doing it. Then slowly over time, you will be surprised to find that one day you have land, you're growing your own food, making your own jam, etc....you're a homesteader from the city. You don't need to know HOW you're going to get there, just start one step at a time and it all unfolds in due course.

As you develop this connection, you have the power to rebuild yourself into the version that you want to be. You can meet yourself with love over and over again, which encourages your inner spirit to show you where there's work to be done and how you can get there in your own way. You can develop a deeper intuition to know when things aren't for you and when they are, and over time this creates more trust within yourself. As you follow your intuition and create this connection you are also creating more safety within the body and regulating the nervous system. You're letting the body know it's safe to slowly shift out of PTSD mode and into a more peaceful way of being in your everyday life. Once you are able to do this, there's so much that you can accomplish for yourself, so much that you can heal or call into your life because your body feels safe to do so.

This is a process that can't be rushed or forced, it has to come on its own time. That inner worthiness is in there, waiting to emerge into your everyday way of being but it takes time to let your body know it's safe to do so. The relationship with the narcissist or emotional abuser has put your nervous system into a state of fight or flight, so once you are able to stop running and stop fighting is when you can develop inner safety. This comes when you're ready to make dramatic shifts in your body, something that I will go into in the next chapter.

One way that I helped myself to develop inner safety within my body, was by putting myself into a safer environment and then repeating to myself over and over for months, "I am Safe." At first, this felt like total bullshit because I'd never felt safe before, but just like how I developed inner worthiness, I created this by repeating it and then continuously putting myself into safe environments. I am a logical person and know that I cannot control the outside world so those safe environments were very often in nature. In this way, it wasn't around people, so no other energies were able to interfere with mine and as I sat in nature I'd repeat "I am safe, I am safe, I am safe."

I'd do this by walking, hiking, swimming, driving to nature, listening to the ocean, etc. Nature soothed my soul in a way that nothing else could and allowed the space for that story to take root and become true. I was safe, I am safe and nature was supporting me through this process to prove to me that I wasn't lying to myself.

I stopped going to bars or other crowded events where people were under the influence of something because let's be real, those environments aren't safe, there's always a fight or verbal altercation of some kind. I stopped sitting in traffic, to drive during low traffic times, I started wearing my helmet on my scooter always because we all know that driving without a helmet is not safe. I wasn't about to lie to myself and I'm not one who follows the "fake it til you make it" saying. I set up my environment to be safe so that I could cultivate the true sense of safety in my body. Then if I was in a situation that felt unsafe by my outside world, I wasn't rattled anymore because I'd re-written this inner dialog. Someone could get into an argument in a restaurant and instead of feeling the need to look for the nearest exit, I'd simply look at this person and think, "Oh they haven't yet developed the tools to manage their emotions" or "Man, he's having a bad day"; I could see it for the truth and the facts, continuing to feel totally safe because it had nothing to do with me.

When you begin reprogramming yourself the movement and repetition of the mantra, both verbally and writing it in a journal helps to reprogram the DNA in the body. You're speaking to your cells with love and respect, they will trust you and heal with you, for you. It sounds so "Woo-woo" when you first start out talking to your body, but it is real...We've all seen the experiment of speaking to the two plants, one plant receives love and kindness and the other plant receives hate and anger.

Which plant dies?

Which plant thrives?

Our bodies are like plants, we thrive in conditions of love and nurturing. When we meet ourselves in this way, and then our cells change! Can you even envision this!? Just like the plant, with met in love, your mind, body, and spirit come together to make powerful shifts into that inner knowing of worthiness and self-love.

Without knowing your story and having a glimpse into mine, I feel confident saying that as a collective we are here to clear the karmic pattern of victimhood to emotionally abusive patterns within our society. We are here to learn to meet ourselves in true love, acceptance, kindness, and compassion. I believe that when we each as individuals develop these emotional muscles to do so our world will dramatically change. Not to some type of place where we all sit around and sing Kumbaya but where we are considerate to those who are healing as we're all on different playing fields. We will release the weight of shame and grief to be able to see past our pain and into our karmic story, releasing it and coming into a space of love for all and acceptance for all.

***

THRIVING EXERCISE:

Take note of yourself as you are now, versus how you were in the relationship with the emotionally abusive patterns or people, has much changed by how you're relating to yourself or the world around you. If your nervous system is in fight and flight mode, will play a big role in how you're showing up and how you're able to show up, being truthful with where your body is helps you to thrive more.

Do you find yourself in a fight-or-flight nervous system? Often feeling the need to defend yourself, short-tempered, argumentative, a "need to get away" or escape your life or even just a room of people, do you have panic attacks?

Do you feel safe in your surroundings?

Do you feel safe in your body?

Do you trust yourself?

What is a story that you are living out that's keeping you in survival mode?

Does the story you stated above have to do with finances, or relationships with friends or to yourself?

Is this story ready to be released from your body?

What new mantra can you tell yourself to help you shift from where you are now in this story, to where or who you want to be?

Write this mantra down in a journal. Write it every day, multiple times a day, and record yourself saying it with conviction and believing it to be true. Allow this new perspective to be rewritten within your body each time a trigger point arises from the old story.

<u>Those around you:</u>
Get really curious and observe those that you're around, without judgment, or shame, how are you relating to the people in your life:

Write down the closest 5 people to and how you relate to them:

Do they encourage you through love or fear?

Do they believe in your healing journey?

Do you support you and your choices?

Do they celebrate you and your wins?

Do they focus on the positive or negative aspect of life?

Have any of them been in a narcissistic relationship? If so, are they healing from it or still in it?

Do they try to control your life for their comfort or encourage you to branch out of your own?

<u>Safety in your body:</u>
Where in your life can you create distance in order to cultivate safety in your body and mind?

Create a mantra that feels good for you to develop safety in your body. Make it short, something you can easily remember on repeat throughout your day, also work through it with intention.

What's a location around you that brings you peace?

How many times per week can you go to this location to recite your mantra?

What's your favorite nature spot around you?

Put into your calendar when you can next go to this nature spot and spot of peace, don't allow anything else to come in the way, within reason, and follow through with the set date and time. Give this space to yourself to begin to really find safety in the body and allow this safety to take root in your worthiness.

When you get into this spot in nature, sit down and just listen to the sounds around you. Go alone and let this be your time.

Hear the nature that surrounds you and allow yourself to just be here for a while, as long as feels good.

When the time is right, remain sitting or walking and repeat this safety mantra over and over as you sit or walk. Shift the energy within your body to begin letting a new story of safety begin to grow so that you can slowly develop your worthiness on top of this safety. When the body feels safe to grow, it will open up for the worthiness to begin coming in.

Do this over and over for many months, set yourself up for this peace and safety. No exceptions or excuses, you deserve this safety, give it to yourself.

<u>Worthiness of love:</u>

How can you begin to see yourself for the amazing and worthy person that you are?

MIRROR WORK:

Sit in front of the mirror and just look at yourself, no words, just really see yourself, without judgments, only your presence.

Notice what happens when you look yourself in the eyes. Notice what happens when you glance across your body. Find your favourite body part and say to yourself, "I love you".

Observe the emotions that arise. Even if you're unable to look at yourself in your eyes...or if the mirror is hard at first, where can you look on your body to say this?

Start small if need be and slowly work your way into looking in your eyes to say, "I LOVE YOU."

Over time this will grow easier and you will be able to recite specifics about yourself that you love or about your accomplishments thus far. Give yourself this gift of worthiness as hard as it will be in the beginning, keep after it and let yourself know, you are fucking worthy of a deep love from yourself, for yourself!

8 |

Ways to Expand on Your Journey

I'd love to share with you some more options of ways to have new and holistic experiences on the journey of healing. Some of the things out there I haven't done as there are thousands of practices, so I'll give you what I've done, I can say it all worked because it all came to me intuitively at the right time and I put forth the effort following the experience to integrate what I'd learned. I did these things when I was willing to make the commitment and follow through, if I didn't feel I could follow through then I didn't do it or haven't done it, yet. As I've mentioned and you'll hear from so many healers, the journey of clearing karma is a process.

Once I began going to therapy all those years ago, it set off something inside me to do better, be better, feel better...all I have wanted has been to feel good. This has taken so much time and places of experimentation and experience, giving me the opportunity to learn so many new things that have totally reshaped and enriched my life.

So far in the book I've talked about....
• Feeling the feels
• Releasing attachments to relationships that are unhealthy
• Re-coding the DNA stories within the body
• Moving through grief & fear
• Developing a deeper connection to your body
• Clearing the karma so it's no longer sticking with you
• Setting boundaries and committing to yourself
• Finding ways to discover and maintain your worthiness
• Meeting yourself in a loving space rather than judgment

Some of the most impactful ways that I have done this are methods of holistic practice that have enriched my life beyond my wildest imagination. There are so many modalities in which to explore and I'm only going to touch on the ones I've had personal experience and the most profound healing from. I trust that some of these will work for you, as well as spark your curiosity to learn more alternative methods to clearing karma and getting out of the shitty patterns.

So often we get stuck in these patterns not only because it's a body memory but because we get stuck in a pattern of grief. Our society doesn't allow us much time to grieve a loss, something that each person needs in order to move forward. The emotion of grief is stored in the lungs, which provides our life force, the breath. So in order to truly make room to breathe, your body and psyche need a lot of nurturing, frequent intentional self-work, and gentleness with the process.

Grief changes you, this is why the divorce or clearing the karma of patterns with a narcissistic relationship had a Before and an After for me, I am not the same person I once was. As humans we deeply fear change, we resist it and avoid it for as long as possible, which keeps us in the loop of the patterns being played out over and over. When you leave a pattern or release an attachment, even when it's in your best interest the body grieves because the story you were living was doing its best to protect you, it needs time to grieve where you were in order to come to where you're going.

Leaving the pattern of narcissistic or emotionally abusive relationships and patterns, causes you to feel physical pain in addition to emotional pain as the body's memory adjusts. Dis-ease in the body is also caused by DNA re-coding, and you'll have many symptoms as your spirit ascends within your body and you develop a higher emotional and spiritual consciousness.

Here are some common Ascension Symptoms:
• Fever
• Nausea
• Dizziness
• Insomnia
• Exhaustion
• Headaches

- Panic attacks
- Cold / Flu symptoms
- Emotional outbursts
- Brain fog/forgetfulness
- Irregular / Irritable bowels
- Chronic or frequent crying
- Plus more serious diseases when these above aren't addressed for long periods of time.

These are all some things that could occur often or intermittently, depending on your body constitution and how deeply you're moving in the work that you're doing. Also, consider your genetics or any chronic disease that the body has been carrying around.

I use the phrase "Ascension Symptoms" to describe what the body's going through, it'll expel those old stories in the form of dis-ease. When we "get sick" the first thing we reach for is an antibiotic, go to the Doctor, take a pill, or anything to make it better fast...this reaction is a programming of our modern Western society. We're programmed and taught to believe that there's some sort of magical pill that cures what ails us...when in reality what ails us is the unprocessed grief and trauma floating around in the DNA. Without having this knowledge, we do what we know, reach for the Pharma, and then expect it to be fixed tomorrow.

When the body is sick or broken, it takes time to heal; your emotional and spiritual body is the exact same way. If you broke your leg, you wouldn't be expecting yourself to take a pill and then walking the next day and the bone to be healed, it needs time. If you did this you'd be causing more damage to the bone in the long run, perhaps needing surgery or developing an infection...apply this to your emotional and spiritual well-being, you cannot bypass or rush the process.

We have been programmed to view these symptoms and many others as a negative thing, immediately reaching for a pill or the Doctor at the first onset of illness. This is a program that keeps us stuck...it prevents the body from doing its natural work with a boosted immune system and prevents the DNA from elevating to eliminate the disease or emotion.

When we take a lot of antibiotics or Pharmaceuticals, this keeps the disease in the body and keeps the body sick, being a repeat customer for the Doctor, not ever getting to the root of the problem. However when we begin viewing these symptoms and others as the body's way of speaking to us, also the body's natural detoxing method, then you won't fear or be concerned for these symptoms to arise. It becomes another method and means to lean into what you're being told.

This being said though, it takes intuition and also caution to objectively look at what's happening in your body to know exactly what you need at any given time. When these "lower level" symptoms of ascension are ignored or repeat themselves for long periods of time they will ultimately develop more serious diseases or injuries that require advanced medical treatment of some kind and radical lifestyle changes, whether you reach out to Western or Eastern medicine is up to you. Allowing yourself to accept discomfort for long periods of time isn't the way your body is meant to operate at its optimum level...I'm very guilty of this as we all are, which is why slowing down to listen is a vital art to learn for your journey.

DETOXING & CLEANSING

There are so so many methods to use for this one, so much so that it can get overwhelming and confusing, causing you to think that the process is hard. I won't lie, it isn't easy to detox or cleanse but it all depends on your perspective and your why, always come back to your WHY when shit gets hard to manage.

I began detoxing and cleansing my body a few years after my divorce, following the breakup that I had with my boyfriend. I first began with Reiki, as I shared this story in previous chapters. These few sessions made such an impact on me that when the same friend who suggested Reiki also suggested Ayurveda, I jumped on the research of finding someone. The Ayurvedic Healer was to help me shift my food and way of relating to myself. At the time I was desperate, I would've done anything anyone suggested, so I'm grateful that the right people came along at the right time, giving me just the suggestions that I needed.

I had spent months crying, sobbing on the floor weeping,

and hugging myself to soothe the amount of grief leaving my body...I felt like I was going crazy. I was properly depressed and looked it, my face was pale and I had dark circles under my eyes. This breakup from my boyfriend, combined with the emotions I was still processing from the divorce and buying my first home had caught up with me. I was in trouble and acting out of character, in addition to all the crying, I was filled with rage and irritability, going off at the drop of a hat. I wasn't sleeping well, was smoking a lot of weed and drinking a lot of alcohol, surrounded by what I thought was eating healthy but was actually too much caffeine, dairy, sugar, processed foods, and tofu. I didn't know this at the time, but now believe that these types of emotions arise when they're ready to leave the body, this level of emotional misery comes into play when you're spirit is desperate to get your attention for a shift in lifestyle pattern.

Once I met with the Ayurvedic healer, every two weeks, she'd slowly adjust my food and give me practices to move through. I had been a vegetarian for many years and learned I was eating too much tofu. The soy in the processed product was throwing off my hormone imbalance causing me to have mood swings and all the crying. She took me off of it cold turkey and added in other types of foods for protein, she put me on all cooked foods, nothing raw, and within one month my life had totally changed! I wasn't crying anymore, I wasn't having the violent mood swings, and was able to think rationally, sleep better and process my emotions rather than staying stuck in the story. I was able to completely let go of the break-up and came into an inner knowing that something and someone was out there who was better suited for me. Following a deep heartache, this is the best place a person can get to.

I worked with her for 4 months and was so dramatically changed following this experience. I was eating what was correct for me, not what was the latest fad and I learned to be able to decipher between intuitive eating and cravings that weren't the best for me. This alone was such a profound way for me to detox that it ended up pushing out infections that had been sitting in my body unnoticed. These infections had been lying dormant in my body because they were a physical symptom of an emotional struggle that I was ignoring and pushing aside for years, with antibiotics and mystery auto-immune diseases...so when I began clearing out the toxins through Ayurvedic eating the dis-ease came out.

About 2 months before I was to leave for Bali for the first time, one side of my face swelled up like I had an orange stored in my check to snack on later, I looked like a cute little hamster. It was crazy to see this! I wasn't in any pain at all but was very dizzy, so it limited me to being home. I of course did what I was programmed to do, and rushed to all the doctors who put me on all the pills, steroid shots, etc. though nothing changed. I was like this for 6 weeks, with a swollen face and laying on the sofa or taking an Uber to meetings.

Finally, after the second visit to my General Practitioner,

he asked, "Have you been to the dentist? Because we've tried everything...so I'm going to also send you for a scan of the face to look for a tumor." The next day I was getting a CAT scan of my face, praying there was no tumor and the following day I was in the dentist's chair...when the dentist exclaimed, "OH MY GOD, and you drove and walked in here??!!" "Ummm, Yesss?" I replied curious as to his dramatic response...a few nurses came in looked in my mouth and said, "Oh my God, sweetie!!"

Turns out, I had an abscess that ran the length of my gum across 4 teeth, I didn't feel a thing! Abscessed teeth are usually excruciatingly painful and very problematic to the health of the tooth and jaw, gone untreated it can lead to reconstructive jaw surgery. He immediately sent me to an Endodontist, who did more scans to discover that I had an infection that had been in my gum following a botched root canal, seven years prior to this!! So for seven years, a piece of root remained in my gum and slowly built an infection as the dead root decayed inside my gum. Through my detoxing, it pushed the infection out of my body. I was placed on more antibiotics and steroids, and surprise surprise, after being on them for 6 weeks already were not working.

The Endodontist was very adamant that I understood if the infection didn't go away within the next 7-10 days, I'd be looking at extensive jaw bone surgery to clear the infection and prevent it from spreading and destroying the bone, or worse going to my brain. In addition, I'd lose the tooth and the ones on either side and be looking to be in the dentist's chair for the next few months. I was petrified! She told me, "I don't want that to happen, I want to know you're on your trip having the time of your life in Asia, so let's do everything we can to get your mouth healthy." She asked me about my emotional state if I'd been depressed or doing anything differently in my life, so encouraged me to examine myself and see what could be emotionally causing the issue. I liked her immediately for suggesting this, it's very rare for Western doctors to go this route so when they do, I trust them and do my homework.

I went home with more steroids, that I ended up not taking. Instead, I mixed a mouth rinse of Doterra essential oils of OnGuard and Tea Tree with warm salt water. I had looked up in my new metaphysical book, and as I was doing the mouth rinse 4-5x per day, I would recite the mantra written from the book that related to "teeth".

According to the book, an Abscess is caused by the emotional turmoil of having fermenting thoughts over past hurts, feeling slighted, and desiring revenge. Admittedly so, I deeply felt this for both of my exes, I was low into the victim mode at this point...however changing my diet, changed my energetic vibration within the body so I was operating at a higher frequency. So the thought process and disease were ready to get out, my body didn't want to harbor that resentment anymore. I combined this with meditating 2 hours per day, doing yoga, journaling all my feelings working strongly with the energies of the earth's elements, also not drinking alcohol. My Ayurveda healer gave me an herbal tea to drink, along with a lot of bone broth and collagen...all of it helped.

It was 10 days later when I went back to the Endodontist, who examined my gum and said it was the healthiest gum she'd ever seen! She asked me what I did and I told her, as I just described. She shook her head and said that was the exact regimen she would've given me if she was legally allowed to refer out holistic practices. She herself practiced this for herself but wasn't allowed to share it with any patients, because she could lose her license. She was both shocked and disappointed that she couldn't share with her patients and so grateful that I took it upon myself to do the research and empower myself through the process.

Following this, I have had zero issues with my teeth, that one in particular. I had been using the oils for years as a way to clean the air in my home, or clean with more natural products, but I had yet to need them for something medicinal and it worked! I can't say that this will work every time for everyone, nor am I recommending this for every tooth infection, I legally am not allowed to say these things either, but I am going to share my experience. I share my experience with oils and Ayurveda because I know that plants work magic when you're following your intuition and when you're listening to your body.

Plants combined with a strong mind, have more healing

power than any pharmaceutical drug on the market. I firmly believe this to always be the case. Many will argue with me and that's okay, it's all about where you're putting your faith. Western medicine is only a few hundred years old whereas earth medicine is thousands of years old from cultures worldwide...it's something that feels more resonate for me. I appreciate Western medicine for what it is and I'm sure it's helped many people, in my personal experience it's never helped me so this is why I hold the opinion that I do. Take it or leave it, remember, "Opinions are like assholes and everyone's got one".

Needless to say, a few weeks following my tooth repair, I was feeling emotionally and physically free! I was on the next flight to Bali and my seven months traveling throughout Asia.

In the years following this event, I have worked hard to clear my body of toxins, doing many types of detoxes, both guided by a professional and self-guided by my intuition. Each one has enriched my life more and more. I stopped getting angry at my body for getting sick and began to stop or slow down to listen to what it was saying. I'd look up my symptoms in the Heal Your Body book and within hours or days, I'd be back on track using the power of my mind and all-natural herbs & oils.

In order to clear the karma, and to change the DNA to fully leave the pattern the body needs to begin getting more and more clear. This allows you to access a deeper relationship with yourself and a better one with others, with nature, and with the food you eat. Your intuition strengthens, your nervous system calms, and you begin to feel truly safe in the body despite the stressors around you. Clearing out the body of toxic waste, both gained in this lifetime or passed down to you, will only benefit you in the long run for so many things. You'll be able to no longer cope with life but thrive and manage it accordingly as it unfolds, there's no greater depth of sovereignty than having a hold of your own health.

This is just one story of triumph over my health, but to be honest, if I told them all, that would be a whole other type of book. I have spent years putting my health first following this incident and it's only benefited me. My hormones have fluctuated for years, and instead of feeling shame for myself, I have been able to take action and follow through in a holistic pattern.

Your health is your wealth, it's the one thing that's so valuable, it cannot be taken away unless you choose to give it away. Reprogramming your body in a healthy way will make you stronger in mind, body, and spirit. It will give you the space to deepen your relationship not only with yourself but with the Great Spirit, God / Goddess, the Universe, or what-ever name you'd like to use, this connection will undoubtedly grow stronger. I've known people who have dedicated their lives to genuinely following through with their health. They are the happiest and most connected to Source that I've ever known, they are truly beautiful people to be around.

As the body stores patterns and ways of thinking, this is the leading cause of why you are not able to leave a pattern or more easily change your mindset. When the body and environment are filled with toxins, then so are the mind and emotional body, they work hand in hand with one another. When you clear the body of toxins, you can clear the mind more easily to shift your perspective, give a confidence boost, and feel better about yourself overall. This helps you to shift out of the pattern more and more or once and for all.

For clarification, when I mention "Toxins", I'm referring to toxins caused by parasites, processed / fast food, meat, dairy, fish, chemicals or cleaning products, candles or scented plug-ins, pharmaceuticals, heavy metals, vaccines, antibiotics, Wi-Fi, abuse, anger, manipulation, stress, anxiety, fear...all of this builds in the body over time when the body is unable to detox itself fast enough. The body has a natural method of detoxing, but when we are consuming these things more consistently then the detoxing process slows down and all the shit builds up in the body. Instead of the body being able to naturally detox, it reabsorbs the toxins and the body, mind, and spirit become toxic, fucking up your nervous system, and digestive tract, suffering from pain or discomfort, mental or physical illness, etc.

You have the power to heal your body with your mind, to be able to achieve that deeper connection to yourself, find safety in the body, and clear the karmic patterns. Once you decide to take the step to get your health in order and follow through then the discomfort slowly goes away. It gets easier to manage life, you feel less stressed, you feel more confident, you feel happier, and no longer live in fear, anxiety, or depression.

The choice is yours and will always be there when you're ready for a lifestyle change and willing to put in the effort to make it happen. You ultimately get to this point, because like I've said we as humans resist the fuck out of change and detoxing is big change… we arrive at this point once you hit that space of being so sick of your own shit. I mean you're so tired of feeling like shit, crying all the time, being angry or easily triggered, or knowing that there's something holding you back and there's no one to blame, it's up to you to take the responsibility for yourself. This is the moment where you end up cutting the shit and get down to deeper work on yourself, when you just can't stand it any longer.

You can relax, you can surrender to the change, and accept that like the seasons change so do you and your life cycles. Nothing is meant to stay the same, nothing is meant to hold on to dead weight as we tend to do. When you learn the art of letting go and surrendering, then you can find joy and excitement in the change.

The main reason why not detoxing causes so much harm is because the body is meant to detox itself. However, like I mentioned when toxins are being piled on and not detoxed then it becomes harder for the body to do its best work. When the toxins are unable to detox the body just reabsorbs them.

Take a look at mucus, we view this as disgusting yet it's such a cool part of the body's detoxing system, mucus builds throughout the body to encapsulate the toxins and disease that enter the body from an external environment. When the mucus cannot detox naturally then you end up reabsorbing that mucus and what it holds, for more mucus to build trying to catch what's being reabsorbed, and it snowballs, it gets bigger and bigger with more and more toxins and the body is just absorbing it all because that's what it's meant to do. The same thing happens in the intestines and colon when you get constipated, if you're not eliminating waste at least 2x per day, your body is reabsorbing the waste causing the disease to build. Detoxing and promoting this process in the body is one of the best things you can do for yourself in order to clear karma and old stories.

Here are some types of detoxes or cleanses to look into:

- Mucus Detox
- Intestine & Colon Cleanse
- Decalcifying the Pineal Gland
- Liver, Gallbladder, Kidney Cleanse
- Womb Cleanse ~ for yeast, UTI, and toxic energy
- Parasite cleanse ~ highly recommended for everyone
- Candida Cleanse and balancing the microbiome in the gut

- Heavy Metal Detox ~ takes years, we have had this one for generations
- Pharma or Vaccine Detox / Cleanse ~ if you're on meds consult your Doctor (Western and Eastern)
  Methods of Detoxing, Cleansing & Rejuvenating (always consult a professional to get you started on the right path for you):
- Qigong
- Kambo
- Ayurveda
- Minerals
- Enemas
- Krya Yoga
- Essential Oils
- Supplements
- Psychedelics ~ with a guide
- (TCM) Traditional Chinese Medicine

My best recommendation for beginning or continuing this process is to contact a professional in the Ayurveda or Traditional Chinese Medicine realm. Both of these are ancient Eastern practices that are thousands of years old and, in my opinion, more accurate than modern medicine in how to deal with the body. Work with practitioners who are well versed in what they're teaching and have been studying it and embodying the work that they are teaching. Stay mindful of fads such as juice fasting and interment fasting, these practices are mainstream and can be very harmful for your body, this works for some people but not all and it only works during certain times. So be vigilant and do extensive research for yourself, it's overwhelming but by just staying away from "fad dieting" will help you to narrow down what's right for you.

If you're interviewing healers for this position, don't be afraid to ask them how long they've been in business, about their certifications and schooling (very important here), and how embodied they feel they are. Get specific, ask about their daily practices and which ones have helped them the most. There are many people out there in these fields, and some don't know jack shit about it, they are just good at selling. This is your time, your health, and your financial investment for yourself. The person you choose should feel right to you and should be practicing what they preach.

It might take a little time to find the right person, but this will allow you to lean into the practice of trusting the process, and knowing that when the student is fully ready, the teacher will appear. It's that simple when you have faith in the process and stop controlling the situation your partitioner will pop up and you'll know it's the right path for you.

WORKING WITH THE BODY INSTEAD OF AGAINST IT

As you learn to let go of resistance and lean into trust, you also begin to listen to the body better rather than fighting against what it's telling you. Energy work and bodywork are profound ways to help you understand how energy flows through the body and how you're affected by the world around you, the food you eat, the patterns you hold, etc.

I've mentioned Reiki, this one is so special to me that I also have been Reiki and Traditional Chinese Medicine body work certified. It's something that I do for myself when I need a shift in energy and also something I'm frequently paying other professionals for as well because it's nice to have assistance to adjust the body's energy.

When I've gotten physically sick or emotionally strained, I go for acupuncture, massage or Reiki...depending on what my body is telling me that I need at the time. Each one of these helps to release stuck emotions and allow the blood to flow more freely, increasing the vibrational energy in the body. Therefore, increasing your mood and your discernment to be able to rest, be present, or be productive.

I've learned through this process of healing the body that the cells in the body are tired, they're exhausted from holding on to so much shit, pushing through, eating improperly, living in chronic stress, all the things that we as people have endured as an accepted way of life. So when you're in the healing journey it's important to have energy work to help repair the cells, let them rest, and accept where your body is on the journey.

Emotional pain is stored throughout the body and the organ system, so taking care of the physical body to the best of your ability is imperative for your spiritual growth and karma-clearing process. In my experience, I've struggled more when I'm not taking care of my body. This is true for everyone but many of us are not aware of how our lifestyles are impacting our lives. Working with one of these types of practitioners or healers are then able to reflect back to your knowledge that you may not have yet and a perspective that's different from yours, showing you your blind spots.

Acupuncture & Traditional Chinese Medicine (TCM) is the best thing that I've done for myself and my body to date. It's not only the needles that penetrate the meridians of the body, to balance the organ function, relieve pain and stress, or drain sinuses; it also comes with herbs that help assist this process following the session. During my marriage was when I decided to get off birth control and following my break up, I got off of it completely, this was around 33 years old. I'd been on it for close to eighteen years at this point and it did nothing but debilitate my health. The procedure of acupuncture and herbs helped me to balance my hormones which took off and on 6 years to get through. I wasn't consistent with this method until I was 37 and then spent 2 years in a regimen that's made all the difference. I now know how to identify when my hormones are out of whack, and the foods and herbs needed to help me get back into alignment. It's truly a Godsend for bodywork in my opinion.

Many people don't like needles...so guess what! TCM has acupressure, which doesn't involve needles, but a pressure applied to the meridians to align the body. Same herbs and same regimen recommendation but without the fearful discomfort.

We hold so many emotions and traumas in the body so finding what works for you through your healing journey is so important. Finding a holistic practice can be considered fun if you're open to new experiences and trying new things objectively. Sometimes something will work at one point in your journey and not at another, this is normal as the body and mind grow and heal. While other things will be something that you stick with for many years to come it becomes your second-nature go-to when you need it. Be patient with this process of working on your body and finding what works best for you, take breaks when needed and always do your research.

Grief and trauma are held in the body in the Root Chakra, the hips for all of us, and additionally the womb for women. When working through bodywork, there are many offerings from practitioners to clear out stories in this area of the body. There are De-armoring massages for the groin or sex organs, pressure points to know about to relieve stuck emotions, somatic movement therapy, or adjusting the food, certain mantras or meditations. There's so much that I can't even put it into one book, nor have I yet had the experience of it all, I do what I'm being called to at any given time. This is my recommendation for you, do what feels right and what you feel excited to try. Sometimes it'll be scary as it will push your edges, and bring you to a point where you feel nervous, scared, or want to cancel the sessions...when this happens check in with yourself, and discover if you're in fear or if its intuition...can be both so being aware of this helps as you're moving through the processes. Be vulnerable, talk to your practitioner about any reservations, they may be able to ease your mind a bit.

Allow yourself the space to work with and listen to your body, over and over again. It will not let you down or lead you astray, it will guide you in the direction that you're willing to go in. Sometimes your mind won't be ready but your spirit will be, sometimes the spirit is ready and the body is too tired to make the move. Knowing when it's time to rest and when it's time to move through deeper work, and knowing the difference will assist you in not reaching burnout, which can happen when clearing trauma.

Be sure to always take time to enjoy your life!!! So many get caught up in the healing journey that they forget to put it all down and just deeply enjoy life, have fun and play.

RE-PROGRAMMING A PAST LIFE STORY

Whether you believe in past lives or soul reincarnation or not, your body is still holding on to past life stories, from your ancestors. I have done several types of journeys in my time over the years to access this part of my psyche to be able to re-write a story that my DNA and psyche have been carrying for a long time, since before I arrived on the planet.

You can access these points through several modalities, Hypnotherapy, Shamanic Journey, Past Life Regression, Akashic Records readings, Psychedelics...this is to my knowledge but there may be more. Within these journeys have been where I've discovered some pretty profound stories that I was carrying or allowing to block me from finding my worth and love for myself. Each modality in its own way gets into the psyche of a past life to receive messages, release pain and trauma, better understand the self, and let go of attachments held from these lifetimes.

I've tried each of these multiple times and every one offers a new story of myself and another attachment released so that I can step into my worth more and more. One journey that helped me to overcome the fear of moving to Bali, was having a Past Life Regression session with a guide. She led me into four lifetimes and each one revealed an attachment that I needed to let go of in order to truly know my strength for this move. The final one was helping me to overcome the fear that I was entangled in, fear of moving, fear of letting others down, fear of what was going on within the world....just a whole bunch of fear!

In the final life that she guided me through, I was taken almost to an apocalyptic, dystopian time frame where nothing was as it seems today, there were fewer people and everything around me was abandoned. Nature was beginning to take over, as vegetation crawled up the sides of vacant buildings and abandoned cars, I was there standing in strength. Within this vision, I was standing in front of what appeared to be some large galleria-type mall, with busted-out windows, and silence all around, I was the only one standing there. Listening to my surroundings, watching out across the distance, for what, I don't know. A small group of people showed up, they were all standing around with me, each of us encouraging the other one...it was revealed to me that I was the leader. I was the person that this small group was looking to for guidance through this abandoned terrain.

Up until this vision through the Past Life Regression session, I'd been told by a few people that I was a leader, something I'd never thought of myself as. Through witnessing this scene I could feel in my body what it feels like to be a leader, a pioneer, and to step out against the grain, to go into the unknown with confidence and a knowing that "Everything was going to be okay." I felt proud and honored to lead this small group and grateful for their trust.

Within this session, as I was able to feel the deep waves of emotions that I was feeling from this vision, I was able to let go of the fear of stepping forward. I was seeing that I wasn't alone as I felt that I was, I would make a small community and it would be like-minded people who were there to support one another. That no matter what happened, I would have and do have people in my life who are supporting me and have my back.

This was it! This was the encouragement that I needed to move forward towards my calling to live in Bali. I was able to feel the fear release from my body and allow the confidence and inner knowing to take over, giving me the strength to hold steady in my plans though I was faced with months of back-to-back challenges. This was something that no one else but another version of me could give myself. No amount of encouragement or story from another person was going to help in this scenario, I was scared shitless and needed to know that I had my back. This session gave me that knowing and I am so grateful for it!

Every one of these sessions for me has been different, and they'll all be different for you as well. So it's something to go into open-minded, ready to receive, ready to surrender, and ready to rise because you sure as hell will release something holding you back to open up to gain in many different ways.

I've learned that through all of these types of sessions, it helps to have developed the safety in the body beforehand, otherwise you end up trying to control the situation out of the inability to yet feel safe in your body. Without the sense of safety, you don't want to let go of control because the psyche and body are communicating that letting go of control isn't safe...this is really important when doing work, have the sense of safety and strengthen it over and over.

PSYCHEDELICS

The use of psychedelics is on the rise again in the West for clearing trauma, not only as a means of partying as we were programmed. Psychedelics are classified as a Class 4 Drug from the US government, making them one of the most dangerous "types of drugs" out there. Or is it?

Using plants as psychedelics as a means to access deeper parts of the psyche and contact inner versions of the self, to clear trauma, and to connect with the Spirit, are practices that have been used through Indigenous and Ancestral Cultures for centuries. The USA labeled these plants as drugs, making them illegal because people in the 1960's were taking a lot of them, and beginning to see the truth through their programming. The rebellion against the establishment caused the government to take this action because they now had thousands of people refusing to take part in the system, protesting political wars, and burning bras to say the least...they were waking up through the use of these plants. The establishment wants people who follow the programs laid out so that we are all falling in line like "good citizens". When we go against this, they are quick to find fault and shut it down. However, through recent developments and people really fighting back this go round, more and more governments are slowly working to legalize some psychedelics to help PTSD patients.

There are different types of psychedelics, Peyote,

Ayahuasca, Magic Mushrooms, Iboga, and many more; each one from a different region of the world and each one accessing a different layer of the psyche to reach the higher levels of consciousness. You walk away from these experiences a different person and will be a different person if you have the willingness and guidance to follow through with the messages given.

Each experience is different for everyone. It's important when considering these plants to begin by working with a guide. They will be able to assist you through the journey, through the experience of going deeper into the realms of what you'll never see with the naked eye. These plants do cause trauma to be released from the consciousness, sometimes when trauma is released, it's helpful for you to have a guide so they can support you through it in a calm and collective way. Anxiety and fear can quickly build in these containers, so having someone present who is trauma-informed and can help you will be a more impactful experience.

There are many group activities in these realms and to this I suggest joining one of the group containers solo, not always with someone you know. This will prevent you and your friend from forming codependency, shame, or fear when you're having your experience. You then won't lean on your friend but will instead learn to lean on yourself and your guide.

Your guide should be someone you trust and has a good

reputation. You are going into a space where your spirit is wide open, boundaries and guidelines should always be established before the ceremony with the plant medicine. If no one mentions this, speak up! Set your own boundaries to build more safety for yourself within this container. Feel good about what you're doing, and feel confident even if there's a little bit of fear, this is totally normal. Listen to your intuition, for whatever reason this doesn't feel right for you then don't participate, you are under no obligation to do so. Always communicate your needs, and your Shaman, if they're good will listen to you, hear you, and respect your wishes. They may question your motives for backing out but under no circumstances should they pressure or guilt you into the ceremony, this is a major red flag, if this happens, walk away.

Personally, I haven't tried all of the plants, it's not something that calls to me but I am a huge advocate for this when it calls to others. The one psychedelic that calls to me is the Magic Mushrooms, it's something I enjoy learning about and working with others on as well. I've studied how to be a guide in this realm before there were courses teaching people to hold this space. I thoroughly enjoy holding this space for another person as it's a gift or calling of mine to do so.

Magic Mushrooms grow globally, unlike other psychedelic plants which are region-specific. Of course, all the mushrooms are different varying from location to location but I believe this is Spirits gift to man, a way to access the psyche and deconstruct the programs and stories we carry. It's a way to open up to the higher self and relieve yourself of the pain and struggle that has encapsulated your spirit for so long.

My first experience of taking Magic Mushrooms was while I was living in Amsterdam, a very appropriate place to answer the call of this plant. Mushrooms had been calling me for many years to access these parts but I wasn't ready or willing to answer the messages that would come through. So I did them when I felt ready and when my body felt safe to surrender to the higher power of these plants and their way of communicating, this was about five years after I began getting curious about how this works.

I was with a boyfriend at the time, who's Dutch, we bought the mushroom truffles and took a weekend out of the city and into the Dutch countryside. It was newly spring, but we were still in a loose lockdown through the global shut-ins, only Germany could travel to The Netherlands at this time. So many people were flocking to the countryside on the weekends, the city would empty out as everything was closed, except beautiful nature.

We rented a car and drove a few hours outside of the city to camp and get reconnected to nature, taking the truffles along. On the day we took the mushrooms, we packed a picnic lunch, plenty of water, blankets, and pillows...we had found an empty field surrounded by woods that we were going to lay in for our trip. We set up our picnic, turned on some soothing music, and consumed the truffles. The experience was soft and gentle, nothing heroic or wildly breakthrough, something to more deeply tap into the self.

While within in this experience, I had two profound things happen for me. When I had some anxiety begin to develop, I closed my eyes and followed the anxiety, asking it what message it had for me, asking, "Why was the anxiety staying in my body?" I've been a person who's always suffered from anxiety (housed in the spleen) because I naturally have low spleen energy, something I found out working with a TCM practitioner. As I followed the anxiety it presented itself as an orange worm, wearing a black top hat, a Bolo Tie like cowboys wear, and carrying a cane…at first it presented as a little jokester, weaving its way inside my body. I was having a physical symptom of a cramp in the left side of my intestine, a pain that I'd felt off and on for most of my adult life.

I grew annoyed following this well-dressed worm around my body, it wanted me to chase it laughing as it avoided my questions. So I took the lead, I stopped chasing this creature and said, "I won't chase you, I demand you to tell me why you stay in my body." Just then the creature turned around, its jokester demeanor gone and it grew larger in a flash, its eyes glowing red and it growled, howled, snarled at me with this giant open mouth filled with Piraña teeth, layers upon layers of sharp teeth. It scared the shit out of me! But I bowed up like a proper Texas woman and screamed right back in its face, it got smaller and I said firmly, "You no longer have power over me, get the fuck out of my body." And just like that, it shrank and a puff of smoke took its place, following this the physical pain was gone, the anxiety was gone and I was filled with a sense of empowerment that I'd never felt before.

This specific incident has come up several more times within a journey to one day reveal that the physical pain represented my power that I was keeping tucked away, the worm was a parasite telling me to stay small. I have been so afraid of my own power that I was allowing myself to play small and keep parasites of fear inside my body to keep me held back in a smaller, "I won't make it" mind frame. Through diligent work, it took me several more years to fully work through the layers of this message.

This is the power of psychedelics when you're working with them intentionally and with a guide. Because I had mentors around me who also used mushrooms, I was able to share this story and ask for guidance over the time that I needed it to help me truly embrace and embody my power, all while consistently detoxing parasites from my body for the next 3 years. This parasite was no longer having control over my body, mind, and spirit that it had been doing since I developed the pain around fourteen years old.

Another message that came through for me during this time was that of a strong spiritual gift that I have, that of Psychic Abilities. Everyone has this, for some, it comes more naturally than others and some are very open to it, most people are afraid of these gifts because they don't understand them.

What we call "Women Intuition" or "A mother knows", is her psychic ability coming out without even being aware of what's happening or acknowledging her full power, as I was not.

The message that came to me was this...as we lay in this field, following the experience with my anxiety I kept getting the strong sense that we weren't alone. So I started telling my boyfriend, "I'm seeing people here"...and I described what I saw...Children running around with dogs, people from another time wearing animal skins for clothes, cooking over fires, and living in huts made of dirt and animals' fur pelts. We were close to a small mound in the grass, and I told him, that people are buried there in a circular pattern, "this mound and field is some sort of burial ground", I said.

He thought my messages were cool and that maybe I was looking into another dimension or timeline. We didn't think too much of it until the next day, when we discovered we had been lying in the middle of a hiking trail. It entered the woods from one side of the field, wove through the woods, and exited the other side of the field, to walk across the field and re-enter the woods opposite for another trail. So naturally, we walked the trail! During our walk we came across this large board with photos, describing the history of the land we were hiking.

As it turns out, the field we were lying on during our trip was absolutely an accent burial ground! The mound was the burial site where the people were buried in a circular pattern layer by layer until the top of the mound was reached.

They would then repeat this pattern in another location. This group of people was living in AD times, a nomadic group who traveled between the land of Germany and The Netherlands, frequently coming back to this space for burial ceremonies that would last weeks or months.

We were floored! We both looked at one another and burst out laughing! In complete joyous disbelief that while on mushrooms I'd picked up every detail that was printed out on the historical bulletin board. My boyfriend looked at me and said, "I knew you were psychic the whole time!!"

You'd be very surprised how much is revealed to you when you move through one of these journeys. You'll be shown not only where to clear the stories but also your gifts, your next steps in life, your love, power, and worthiness. You'll be shown how much you're supported by the Universe at every turn and you'll feel it! Psychedelic journeying with a trusted guide is recommended for when you're nervous system is ready and when you feel a large amount of safety within the body and trust within yourself and Spirit, this is when the messages will be life-altering.

There are some contraindications with this, it shouldn't be done as a way to bypass your emotions and the hard shadows to process. It shouldn't be done when you're in the wrong frame of mind, your mindset needs to be that of optimism, and clarity before entering this space. You can easily get stuck in this routine as a way to connect to Spirit and yourself, that's not what the medicine is for, it's a vehicle for you to use to deepen that connection, remember how it feels, and cultivate that feeling while sober every day in another capacity.

Micro-dosing mushrooms is a way to assist you in overcoming grief and depression. In this case, it's always good to start with a professional guide and do your own research for the best options for you. It's the wild west out there with psychedelics, there's little research, modern medicine doctors don't know a lot and it's only new where the USA is building some treatment centers. This is something that over time you can learn to do on your own at home, maybe purchasing a class or getting a trusted friend to teach you.

If you decide to Micro-dose mushrooms or another psychedelic for depression please understand this is not to replace any pharmaceuticals you may be taking. The programming to consume pills for depression, anxiety, sleeplessness, etc. is, that you have to take the pills daily and for long-term use. This is not true, this is how you become a repeat customer to the Doctor because he sells you on this program. However, Pharma itself isn't meant for long-term use, it's meant for a short-term fix combined with adjusting your food, seeing a therapist or life coach, and doing deep internal work to get to the source of the depression. If you've been on pills for years, consult a different doctor, or multiple doctors of the East and the West on this topic, find one who will truly help you get rid of the depression or whatever ails your long-term Pharmaceutical use.

The micro-dosing is to be used in the short term combined with all I listed above, food adjustment, journaling, therapy, movement, etc....not to be taken daily in place of the pills without addressing any of the actual issues. Get to the root of your emotional trauma and pain to clear the karma otherwise the pills or micro-dosing are just bandaids and temporary fixes.

Psychedelics are not something to jump into lightly. We've abused them in the party scene and this is disrespectful to the plant. Personally, I believe they're meant for intentional ceremony not escaping or enhancing an experience. Perhaps taken with small groups of trusted friends, is this an enjoyable way to connect with nature or those around you. I've personally never understood the attraction for partying around people, alcohol, dark enclosed spaces...ugh it sounds miserable to me! To each his own but you're setting yourself up for more trauma and discord within your body when you participate in this type of scene.

Psychedelics have a negative narrative to them because they are so commonly used in the wrong setting. When you're not in the right frame of mind, with the wrong crowd, combining it with other party drugs or medications it can cause psychological harm and welcome in dark energy or spirits. This is when people typically see crazy, traumatizing stuff which can cause more psychological damage in the long run, instilling fear in the process. Be mindful of your psychedelic use, respect the plant, respect your body, and respect the spiritual message coming along for you from Spirit in the right time and setting.

TIPS, TRICKS, & HERBAL RECIPIES

Connect to a Higher Realm

Whether you've grown up in a religious household or are just discovering spirituality, both of these roads have one thing in common, the connection to a higher realm. Discovering and connecting to a higher source helps you to know you're not alone in this journey, because there will be times when the people in your support system won't answer the phone, they'll be busy and they'll forget to call. This is the human experience of living out its day-to-day and just simply being.

Your Higher Source will not ever be too busy to show you love and support, so locating this that feels right for you, will always be there when you need that validation. There are ways to connect to nature, your healed ancestors, guardian Angels, Saints, Spirit Guides, etc. You will have the opportunity to meet these guides through specific meditations or workshops that will guide you in this direction. You might see things that don't make sense and that's okay, go with it.

Your guides might also shift as well, they come to you during certain periods of your life and will stay with you until you are up level and need a different form of guidance. Even when this happens, they're always there to call on in the future but may not be omnipresent for you if you're not working with them specifically.

For example, there are many guides to work with for opening the heart chakra and connecting more deeply to love, releasing blocks. This can come in the form of the plant Rose, the Egyptian Goddess Hathor, or the Hindu Goddess Ganesha to remove obstacles. When you are focusing on these areas, these guides will help you to find yourself surrounded by love and support.

These are specific examples because above these guides is the One Source or God or Spirit or The Universe, this is the source with which you can connect at any time. This is a source that is within you and is a part of you so as you deepen your relationship with yourself you will deepen your relationship with the higher source.

If working with your ancestors is something that feels right for you, to connect to your roots then you want to be mindful to work with healed ancestors. Many of our traumatic karmic patterns are passed down through the ancestral line, so you don't want to ask just anyone for help, it needs to be an elder who's done healing work. They will show themselves to you when the time is right, you might get a name or an image but when you ask specifically for a "Healed Ancestor" the right one comes forward.

In my experience this can even be children, a healed

ancestor isn't always an elder or older person to you...it could easily be a child. When I was opening up in my life to find more play and connect to my inner child a cousin of mine who died when we were children came forward. He was mentally & physically disabled in his human form and when we were children I thought he was so cool, we often played with glow sticks in the dark or lay in the grass to watch the clouds...when I was connecting to this part of me he came forward to me completely whole and showed me things we did as children for me to connect to. He didn't stay with me too long, but just long enough to guide me in directions of more childlike play.

Stay open in this realm but be clear and specific, only ask for healed guides and guides who represent, truth, honesty, love, and your highest good. You do not want guides coming forward who mask themselves and will lead you in the wrong direction, this does and can happen. Stay vigilant in this area and if it doesn't feel right, then it isn't right! Listen to your intuition always.

Movement
It's important to have regular movement in order to process and allow the emotions to be released from the body. If you're one who likes to go to the gym, then also add something that helps with flexibility, Yoga, Thai Chi, Qigong or Pilates.

A movement that promotes flexibility helps you to release

the emotions that have been stored in the physical body, the fascia, and the joints. Getting the flexibility to these areas lets you connect deeper to the body and become more flexible in how you're showing up in life. If you find your body hurts, is stiff when you wake up or is stiff when you slow down then this is indicating stuck emotions.

Get creative with yourself! If the above doesn't appeal to you, go for a walk, put on your favorite music and dance it out, swim, or hike...the options are endless when it comes to movement, just get out there and do it! Do it regularly as part of your healing process, work up to daily if its something that's new for you.

Movement as we all know helps to reduce cortisol, the stress hormone, and increase endorphins, the hormone that gives your mind an optimistic outlook. The movement is vital to your emotional, physical, and spiritual health, in addition to truly increasing the strength of your mind. Even when you don't feel like moving, do it anyway, something low-key or short-lived is okay from time to time, just stay consistent in the intention of movement for mind, body, and spirit.

Some of my favorite yoga poses, that help to get a full body stretch, calm the mind and get you centered into your breathe are:

Plank Pose – (you can YouTube how to do this, if it's

new), start small and work your way up. No need to be the hero here, you're building strength with this one.

Down Dog - also options on YouTube to stretch the whole body and is known to reduce stress within minutes.

Legs up the wall - this one is so nice to release tension and emotions from the hips and lower body, it also helps your body to relax for a better quality of sleep. Doing these poses with slow intentional, deep breaths assists you to connect to yourself, calm the mind, listen to the body, and feel energized when you stand up. Give it some time if its new!

Essential Oil Blends

It's important to consult a professional doctor regarding any health issues and a holistic practitioner regarding essential oils before use. If you have known allergies then do not follow a recipe. These are suggestions and not to replace any medical treatment needed, use your intuition and do your own research before following directions from anyone!

When using essential oils a few things to keep in mind:

- Never apply citrus oils in the sun, they will burn the skin
- Research your oil company first to be sure they use quality produce and do their own testing for safety, etc.
- Don't buy oils online at large box stores, or in the grocery - these oils have toxic carrier oils inside that are dangerous for your body

- Consult a professional before using oils on children or pets
- Use an organic carrier oil such as coconut oil, jojoba or avocado oil
- When ingesting oils be sure they are manufacturered to follow the supplement guidelines or say they are safe to ingest, AKA food grade oils
- Diffuse oils for no longer than 30 minutes at a time to give your sinuses a break, even less time with children or pets present

Emotional Release Essential Oils Blend:

Apply 1 drop each with a carrier oil to the heart chakra (sternum bone)

Diffuse in diffuser:

2 drops - Bergamot

2 drops - Wild Orange

2 drops - Lavender

1 drop - Frankincense

Grief Blend:

Diffuse in diffuser:

2 drops - Ylang Ylang

2 drops - Patchouli

Sleep Blend:

Diffuse in diffuser:

2 drops - Balance Blend from Doterra

2 drops - Patchouli

2 drops - Lavender

Herbs & Holistic Health

Consult an Herbalist, TCM or Ayurvedic practitioner for any supplements or herbs that will be right and specific for you. As you're clearing karma and moving through a transition phase of your life the body can become depleted on minerals and vitamins, so increasing this and changing things out as you go will improve your transition phase.

Often you can get irritable bowel, bloating, nausea, indigestion, etc. regarding gut imbalance as emotions are processing. This is an Ayurvedic tea blend that's good for what ails you in your gut:

Mix 1 tsp of each ingredient into a teapot or French press - can be powder or seeds

- Coriander
- Cumin
- Fennel
- Splash of lime

Steep for a tea-like effect and drink in a quiet place. Allow the herbs to rinse out the stagnant energy and increase the nourishment of your gut. Consult a professional Eastern Practitioner or Western Medicine Doctor for further instructions or care if needed.

Other teas to help calm the nervous system or help you sleep are chamomile or lavender. Note with teas, ones that are sold in grocery stores or in a tea bag often have harmful chemicals in them in order to keep the herbs fresher for longer. If you're going to be an avid tea or herb user, then it's best to consume loose-leaf teas in smaller quantities from reputable sources.

If you desire to have deeper access and to open the third eye during meditations, relaxation, or lucid dreaming ~ Blue Lotus is a beautiful and gentle herb for this. You can find it in tea, tincture, or oil. This herb can be used instead of a psychedelic, it boots dopamine and calms the mind.

There are so many beautiful ways that can enrich and assist your journey to be more smooth and cultivate safety in the body. I encourage you to take some of my suggestions to create something that feels good for you! Do your own research, follow your intuition, and come to the conclusion that's right for you. Because there's so much I can't even begin to put it into this book, so ask for help, share with friends, or reach out to the professionals that I've suggested.

You do not have to do this alone! This is something that I thought for so many years and once I began asking for help I began to see all the support and love surrounding me. It never hurts to ask questions and expand your horizons. Have fun with it! I can't continue to stress this enough, it takes time, it takes patience and it takes gentleness, you deserve to be happy and to find joy. You deserve to cultivate a deep love for yourself that nature and movement can be such a strong support for you.

9 |

Finding Forgiveness

There's been so much shared in this book that I trust you can reference it from time to time for years to come. I pray that this book guides you through some gnarly healing times and encourages you to keep going.

One topic I haven't touched on, one that I don't see spoken about a lot in the healing world and that's Forgiveness. This is a topic that certainly can't be rushed or bypassed, a bandaid can't be put over it to soothe the ache, it has to come with time and come from within. I believe that forgiveness is the medicine that truly alleviates the layer of pain into a whole other realm of higher consciousness. Allowing for more joy and peace to enter the heart to take the place of the hurt, pain, and trauma that was held in that place.

I began this spiritual journey because my goal was forgive-ness. I wanted to forgive myself along with any and everyone whom I felt wronged by. I had seen people in my life who lived a life of un-forgiveness filled with bitterness and resentment, it was sometimes hard to be around these people because they were in so much emotional pain even years after their trauma. You wanted to hold them and assure them everything was going to be okay and it was okay to let go of their resentment but this is the path that everyone reaches in their own time when they choose.

I've watched un-forgiveness eat at individuals like an emotional cancer, slowly taking away the light that was inside them. It always hurts me to see a person in this state, this is sometimes how the cycle of abuse can perpetuate. When one is abused and is unable to find forgiveness, or chooses to not work on oneself to get there, they then become the abuser.

Forgiveness is layered, it happens little bit by little bit through each piece of work that you do. It can take months or years to reach, it has no expiration date and it comes sometimes when you least expect it. When I first called my therapist when I separated from my ex-husband, I told her I wanted to do deeper work on this because I wanted to forgive him. My first layer of forgiveness came when I accepted and forgave him for asking for a divorce.

This allowed me to move into the other layers as time went on, to reach this past year, eight years after my divorce to truly forgive him and others on every layer for telling me that, "I'd never make it". I held on to this phrase for so long, letting it propel me out of fear...I forgave those who said it and I forgave myself for holding it.

I wanted to write about forgiveness and to be honest, I'm still learning about it, learning how to get there and how to share with others. I think the biggest aspect that allowed me the space to heal was accepting things as they are. I've spoken about Karma, past lives, DNA, and mindset shifting, so many factors that I believe to be true, but you may not. You may have totally different viewpoints of these spiritual beliefs and that's okay, regardless of your belief system you can still find acceptance in your life. You can choose to accept that this is where your life has led for one reason or another, you can choose to let go of any resistance that arises in your situation.

Resistance begets un-forgiveness, it keeps you in the loop, keeping you in the victim mindset or harboring feelings of resentment. If you're resisting anything in your life then it's an area that desperately needs your attention, it needs compassion, acceptance, then forgiveness.

Through all of the stories that I've let go of within myself, through all of the shifts that I've been in and welcomed, accepting the flow of it all has allowed me to expand and release whatever I've been holding on to. It allows me to welcome in more of something that's better for me and allows me to see my internal world differently. It's allowed me to release control of my outside environment in order to be able to control what I can, which is myself and my responses to life.

I cannot control another person, and neither can you. We cannot control how others respond to a life we share with them or to a life that's happened for them. We each have the responsibility to govern ourselves. This is why each of us has the power to forgive, the capacity for it and the body begs for the emotional release of forgiveness. I've learned through this process that I can forgive, I can forget, and I can no longer welcome toxic environments in my field. This alone has been huge for me. Not only giving myself permission to let go and forgive but giving myself permission to release that individual, along with the pattern within me. Encouraging myself through the scary parts of letting go of a pattern to welcome something new and better for me.

To share more about this with you, I asked three very important women who are in my life to share their stories of leaving an abusive cycle. These women have all made radical choices in their lives to be able to leave toxic environments and break the cycle for themselves and for their lineage. When they asked me what topic they should write about, I replied, "Please write anything that comes up for you." A few weeks later, I had three emails, with three compelling stories, all about forgiveness.

This was a very Divine topic to complete this book. After you spend years doing your own version of healing work it is enviable that you will forgive yourself and others, that you will view yourself and others or situations that have hurt you with compassion. Without making excuses for the behavior, you just see it differently, more lovingly, more compassionately, and with more forgiveness. Please enjoy these short stories from my therapist, my friend, and my mother...may their stories enrich your life as much as they've enriched mine.

Entry from a Licensed Psychologist:

A priest bestowed the Catholic Last Rites, the Death Sacrament, on me, on the day of my birth. Family, nurses, doctors, and the priest were all preparing for my death.

I fought to breathe. I was in an incubator for a month as my lungs attempted to form. My heart stopped countless times and would through my 1st year of life. I was born into a dark night of the soul, my little body fighting to stay alive, my emotional body struggling to find warmth and security in a mother who felt like ice, lacked empathy, and as an adult, I'd learned, was, and is sociopathic. I came into the world and the world immediately challenged me to fight for life, to persevere, to be resilient, to be able to stay in my earthly body, claiming this one precious life as my own.

This birth experience was the beginning of a life that programmed me to believe life was a struggle. I did what I knew— struggle— just as someone who only speaks one language can only speak that language. I survived life and didn't know how to live it. Struggle was my only language and I've spent two decades unraveling this original teaching and learning a new, artful language of peace, ease, wholeness, worth, and love.

I survived life until 35. Now, I thrive. I love life now. My mind and body now trust me to refuse struggle and invite ease, to live life with as much peace and gratitude instead of as an activated, anxious, hyper-vigilant, nervous nelly. It's been quite the journey.

To escape the cycles of abuse, I had to own my own choices, made out of lessons of constant struggle. I had to 1st look at, then own, my poor decision-making, no matter how understandable. In my youth, I knew better how to make unhealthy decisions bringing more and more struggle than peace. Radical ownership eventually set me free, but felt torturous to see, to own, to admit to myself and the world.

My biological father abandoned me fully by age ten—there had been threats on my life that his fluently Italian self would kidnap me, take me to Italy, and leave me for dead during their divorce. My mother then married a child sexual predator and handed me and my siblings to him, even though she knew he had been accused of sexually abusing his four and two-yearold children and could only visit with them under court-appointed supervision. I lived with my grandparents, my functional parents, for the impactful ages of six to twelve and they died when I was age fifteen and then seventeen, untethering me and solidifying a growing PTSD and supremely raw nervous system and worn-thin self-worth. My abusive stepdad was allowed to adopt me in the same parish (county) that required him supervised visitation with his own biological children. I emerged into adulthood more lost, confused, and struggling than the day I was born. I trusted no one, most of all myself.

My sexual abuse memories were truly repressed while I lived in the abusive home—and this remains controversial in mental health circles. Now, I believe spirit as much as psychology helped repress my conscious awareness and helped block my sexual abuse reality from myself as a teenager and young woman, so I could get out of the parental home of my mother and legal father. Had I consciously known he was crossing Dad's boundaries into sexualized territory for me or my siblings, I very well may have imploded my own life by grabbing the gun kept on the top of the refrigerator for home safety and murdering my parents in rage, defense, and finality for the sexual abuse of my sisters. The fighter in me— created the day I was born—combined with the protective older sibling persona I took pride in—did not have any inkling of how to self protect and yet I owned the protector role with ferocity, I would've done anything to stop my sister's abuse had I consciously known. I have made great peace with how my spirit worked with my psychology to shield me so that I could be here today, so that I could become a force of healing and life-living for myself, and then, for so many others through my work as a counselor, coach, yoga and meditation teacher, and mental health podcaster.

There is no one turning point that directed me away from survival mode and toward thriving. Healing and self-evolution, for me, has been like a coast-to-coast American road trip—so many mini-destinations, left turns, right turns, gas peddle, break, tank refills, and engine maintenance. It's a trip to heal—so much is breathtakingly beautiful like seeing The Rocky Mountains for the 1st time or the Joshua trees in Joshua Tree National Park that grow nowhere else. The moments in life I finally showed up for myself, saying 'Enough!' dripped with similar stunning power and bittersweet beauty.

Like a road trip, I've learned to emotionally and mentally 'Gas-up,' I've learned to push through to make it to the next destination as much as learning to stop, rest, rejuvenate, slow down, and take in the view. This has been slow, deliberate work, letting go of dysfunctional teachings while intentionally seeking and soaking up true wisdom. Slow is good and not a bad thing—good, solid healing is a process of becoming, not a light switch flipped. On the trip of healing, I've done best when I'm moving slowly, a chance to take in all the sights and miss little on the road trip. The slowness that can be so infuriating on a healing journey is actually what allowed me to become a whole and fully integrated person, difficult when any human ego expects to get there yesterday. Patience and kindness, cultivated, with the help of my therapist, my guide, my spiritual sister and mother, have made all the difference.

The 1st turning point in my life I can pinpoint was definitely brought to me by Spirit and it still gives me goosebumps to consider it. After my memories flooded back in my early 20s, when an abusive, narcissistic, male partner attempted to initiate sex with me while I was sleeping. I was able to put together timelines of what happened to me in my youth, I realized Spirit was taking care of me long before I consciously trusted Spirit to be with me. The year I began being sexually abused in my own bed I also read the book, I Know Why the Caged Bird Sings by Maya Angelou. It is her own written story of her own childhood rape. To this day, Maya Angelou remains one of my chosen mothers. I often call her in, and imagine her standing behind me, her hand on my left shoulder, my right hand placed over hers. I have a huge thigh piece tattoo with 3 uncaged birds out of the cage, me, the secret breaker a red bird holding the key. The world may bore us to one biological mother, while the Spirit offers us as many spiritual mothers as we want and need.

As I dated as a young woman, I continued the patterns of abuse and struggled. In the vein of doing what I knew, compounded by the grief of losing my grandparents who were my true parents as a teenager, I was faking life through million-ton depression. My 1st high school boyfriend broke my heart by cheating with a very close girlfriend. I ran away from home in October of my Senior year, couch surfing, bar hopping (it was southern Louisiana and much more normalized to be in a bar as a teenager than anywhere else in the United States), trying lots of drugs, and devaluing my body to allow any man to use it who took interest. I never completed or outwardly threatened suicide as a cry for help but I often contemplated suicide, never wanting to die, but feeling too demoralized, empty, and worthless to live. I trusted no one.

Another turning point was attaining a scholarship that began statewide the year I graduated that covered in-state tuition and gave me a small stipend for food. As an Act of God, I made it into the University of New Orleans and its dorms. Ultimately, I would attain an undergraduate psychology degree and a graduate degree in counseling. The grounding of school was life-saving and gave me an identity as a 'Good Student' when my emotional identity was in the gutter. I could see worth in my achievements before I could see worth in myself—it is sad to look back on, the reduction of a person to achievement, but it gave me a foothold to begin climbing out of low self-worth to eventually be able to be on solid, stable ground.

By Christmas my 1st semester of college, I had been pursued by a man six years my senior at the restaurant I worked. I eventually married him, the emotionally similar version of my mom in male form because we so sadly do what we know until we know better. This is why abusive and predatory types generally target the young. It's easier to manipulate and dominate someone who hasn't yet figured out how to be their own authority figure. At the time, the southern 'Good Girl' dynamics of obedience and people-pleasing encouraged me to door-matting myself in relationships, to give my personal authority away, particularly to those positioning themselves as 'Knowing better.'

By the end of that relationship, I was raw, had spent eleven days in a psychological unit having made the decision to check myself in after I broke the secret of incestuous abuse and pressed charges on my Dad. My husband at the time, in a supreme narcissistic fashion, positioned himself as the victim of my abuse because it made me a bad wife. My awakening appeared, to his way of thinking, as proof that he had a 'Nuts Wife,' and that was not what he had signed up for, nor deserved.

That psychiatric unit visit changed my life. My mom and my 1st husband attempted to team up and master manipulate all staff—and the hospital staff did what my extended family never could and never would—saw them as the manipulators they were and simply, shut that shit down, for my behalf, for the support of me. The staff did something they said they had never done before, they had me read my own psychological evaluation and come into the staffing with all psychologists, psychiatric nurses, and support staff for them to collectively tell me that I was not the problem in my family system. They told me I was smart and I was not manipulative—that the moment I checked in, it was like I could finally take a breath and exhale. They told me I was nothing but helpful on the ward, helping to calm the other patients with kindness and sincerity, I also participated in group and individual therapy with insight and willingness. They also told me that they believed I had been deeply depressed since very young, maybe four or five years old, because my mom was not warm, forgiving, or understanding, something every child needs to feel whole and safe. They also told me that my mom and husband at the time were furious when hospital staff set boundaries and they wouldn't let them manipulate my care or what staff thought about me. They had both tried to convince hospital staff that I was crazy, irrational, an addict, lazy, manipulative, reactive, etc. I certainly, back then, was reactive in the face of being manipulated and I often felt out of my mind crazy—this hospital gave me the most precious life-affirming gift that I desperately needed—that the crazy was outside of me and not inside of me. They saw me as a valuable and worthwhile person at a time when I was starving to know my own value. They saved my life and I think of them often, twenty years later, with tremendous gratitude. I can also own that I saved my own life, too, by being willing to surrender, ask for help, and no longer hide.

Another turning point in my journey came from a professor in my graduate counseling program.

Before going to the hospital I had the composure to send an email to my favorite professor that explained why I would be missing her class that evening as I was self-checking into a mental ward because I couldn't handle my dad's arrest for my childhood sexual abuse, the memories flooding back, my family's reaction. I told her that I was very sorry and sad because this meant I could never be a counselor because I was, well, too crazy. I sent that message before leaving to check into the ward, thinking that my dream of being a counselor was kaput. I read her response the day I was released and wept. It said, "Good for you, Nikki! Everyone should take a mental health vacation every now and then. Take care and come back to school when you get out—this will make you an even better therapist."

I did go back to school. Another turning point was that I didn't hide my experience from my program and honestly shared my experience with the other students. They thought I was brave and strong and inspiring, not pathetic, crazy, or irreparably broken, as I had feared and as I had deep down judged myself with the shame I was carrying.

It took me nine more months to leave my 1st husband. It was not planned well. It was a cliché-ed leaving-in-the-middle-of-the-night only the clothes-on-my-back domestic violence escape. I never went back, in fear of my life. Eventually, the courts gave him a no-contested divorce and I was penniless and homeless, but free.

There's been more. I am a New Orleans native and I was displaced when Hurricane Katrina hit. I've had a 2nd marriage that was less awful than the first but worlds away from healthy. I lost all contact with my stepdaughter from my 1st marriage and grieved her like a mother grieves a wrong and early death of a child. Leaving the in-lawed families I married into ripped scabs off of the wounds left by my bio-logical father's abandonment. In my early 20s, I went fully no contact with my mother and in subsequent years, sadly no contact with my siblings, just too much dysfunction thick between us.

Today, I am happy and whole.

On that seeker's journey, that coast-to-coast road trip to find a life, heal a life, and grow a life, I have come far with much help along the way. My counseling professors showed me to have no shame about my experience or my mental health vacation and that professor was right—I am a better counselor, guide, healer, and person for the experience.

A calling to yoga provided me with a framework to integrate and partner with my body, love it, condition it, and respect it. I've let go of street drugs and pharmaceutical drugs, only using various plant medicines that work with my body's intelligence. Entrepreneurship has challenged and taught me that my authentic self, paired with my integrity for truth, and my strong work ethic given me by my German-descended Grammy, are unstoppable forces. I have manifested a life I love, free of all abusers, full of love and support. My 3rd husband is my rock, he is my biggest supporter. Together, today, we produce a mental health podcast, Emotional Badass: Where Moxie Meets Mindful, and have used my story to help others who have been born into struggle so that they can know all healing is possible when we refuse to give up and just keep putting one foot in front of another.

I am tenacious and I love myself. My inner child trusts

me—the most important person in the world for her to trust. I make decisions that bring my mind and body the respect and peace little me missed out on. I have shed so many layers of hurt and at times, was fearful the layers would be endless. They are not. While I will always be evolving, there is an end to the pain. I take me and my hard-earned wisdom forward every day and every day I am grateful for it all. I have no PTSD symptoms anymore—something doctors told me would be a part of my life forever. Healing is possible beyond what we can imagine. I am here because I kept going. I assure anyone reading—just keep going—it is worth it because you are worth it.

~ Nikki Eisenhauer

Entry From an Energy Coach & Kambo Practitioner

The body is always speaking to you, the question is: Are you listening?

I wasn't listening until I got to Bali.

Bali is said to be the purification center of the planet as there are six purification regions on the island that circulate and cleanse the energetic blood of the earth.

No wonder so many of us on the spiritual path are called to this beautiful island to cleanse and purify ourselves of our past.

Bali first came to me in the dream space. I had never actually even been to that side of the world before, but I was very drawn into these continuous visions and synchronicities that were presenting themselves to me in my reality.

The call grew stronger and stronger until I surrendered, sold all of my belongings, and ventured off to this magical place with two suitcases.

I intended to connect to nature, connect more deeply to myself, and become "embodied," even though at the time I didn't quite fully understand what that term meant.

What I did understand was that I generally spent the majority of my time, "up in the clouds," in my way of thinking and that within my body I suffered from unfixable scoliosis. I use the term "unfixable" because that is what I heard from multiple doctors, practitioners, and chiropractors over the years. I would find myself in these offices multiple times per year to the point where I could not function in my day-to-day life optimally because my back pain was creating intolerable tension in my entire body and occasionally migraines.

The wonderful thing about Bali is that the island prompts you with your next life lesson very clearly and it always seems to align with your intention. I didn't expect two scooter crashes within two weeks would align me with my intention of embodiment, but that was the catalyst for learning what it meant to listen to my body, to heal my body, and to live in my body.

I found myself in an osteopath's office in Canggu one day, because thankfully there were no broken bones from my scooter crashes, but there was however a clicking in my wrist. I was about to leave the practitioner's office when my intuition popped in with a strong hit to ask if it would be possible for her to take a look at my spine and see if there was anything she could do.

The practitioner took a look at my spine, asked me to do a couple of exercises as she observed, and told me that it would require a great commitment, but she thought it was possible to align my spine back to the centre.

This was the first time in my entire life that a practitioner deemed my spine as potentially fixable.

There is a lot that I could dive into around the messaging I received from the medical field as a young child and what the words "unfixable," "deformed," and "crooked," implanted in my psyche, but I feel in relation to Johnna's beautiful work, you can begin to imagine what manifested in the relationship I had with myself.

Through healing my spine I was able to do the deeper work I had always been called to do, but never quite looked at, and that work was the Mother wound.

The metaphysical anatomy of scoliosis is not feeling supported by God/Source/Universe and for me the root of this began when my Mother who was experiencing postpartum depression could not care for me in the way my soul needed upon my arrival to this planet. My spine actually grew its curvature towards the masculine side of my body and away from the feminine side of my body because it felt unsafe in the feminine.

Our body is always speaking to us.

When I found myself inside of that osteopathy office in Canggu, I knew I was finally ready to look at my spine and everything that meant. Sometimes it takes a while for us to arrive at the place we are ready to commit to our healing and no matter when that is it is always the divine perfect time.

The truth is that along my journey thus far there were never the right guides, the resources available or the time to commit and when I found myself in Bali I had all of those things, as well as an ignited warrior spirit.

Each week I attended osteopathy sessions and this was the most challenging and painful work I had ever done. The practitioner, Ali, we will call her, would move my bones back in place without any painkillers. Digging deep into my muscle tissue to align my sacrum, spine, and ribs I was pushed to my absolute limits.

Every time after I had a session I felt lighter, more freer in my body, but only after I went home to process the deep emotional release that needed to happen in order for my muscles to release the traumatic memories they held to allow the spine to remain in its newly aligned nature.

This work was deep, painful, emotional, and deeply spiritual, however, it was my personal pathway to embodiment.

I understood how things like burnout and stress could manifest ailments in the body, but I didn't know how deep metaphysical anatomy went, or in fact that it was and is Truth.

There was one point in the journey of healing my spine where I finally got to a place of full alignment as every single bone was back in its place and Ali told me I could take an extra week in between treatments.

I was over the moon about my win! It was all worth it: the pain, the tears, the money, etc. I was healed! Or so I thought…

Within the two weeks between treatments, I found myself triggered into the story I was not supported by Source, and the muscles in my back seized, pulling my spine back to its original curvature before I began treatment.

Back in Ali's office, she asked, "What happened? Your spine has completely regressed."

Devastated and not fully aware of the results of the emotional trigger I experienced I replied, "I don't know."

"What I can tell you," Ali went on, "is that this is not something physical that happened. This is solely emotional. I can tell this because of the muscles in your back, they have tensed and pulled the spine out of its alignment so this is not something that occurred out of a physical mishap that could have happened, for example, at the gym."

Immediately what came to me was the deep trigger I was experiencing in my reality around not feeling supported by the divine.

"I think I know what it is," I said, "I'll work on it and I'll see you next week."

When I said I would work on it, I meant it. I was fully committed to clearing this pain and discomfort once and for all. I knew I had to go to the root, my Mother.

I hadn't spoken to my Mother in 15 years, but she had in the previous week reached out via Instagram so I had a place of contact for her. I gathered up the courage and sent her a voice note expressing that I forgave her for not accepting me in her life, that I thought about her often, that I loved her, and thanked her for giving me life.

My mother responded by calling me over Instagram and I answered. The version of her I received on the phone was unfortunately the same version I received of her through my upbringing.

"The only person who needs forgiveness here is you." She was drunk and clearly still very displeased with me.

I listened on the phone for thirty minutes as she relayed story after story after story about how her life was great before I entered, how my brother was always the Angel child, how I created so much drama in her life, and how life would be better without me and my father in it.

Holding space for her verbal abuse was enough to put my entire body through an upheaval. I politely said I had to get off the phone, blocked her, and cried all night.

When I say I cried I mean I wailed, I sobbed and I wept from a deep place within my body and soul I had never met before.

The next morning my next step was granted to me through the new spaciousness I created in my body by releasing the suppressed trauma: I would do a specialized Kambo treatment.

Being a Kambo practitioner I have a very powerful connection to the Frog so it was very easy for me to trust this medicine was the next step, even if it didn't fully make sense how a medicine known for its detoxification of the body would support me in my deep emotional release.

Because I would be unable to physically place the Kambo points along each chakra in my spine I called on my dear friend and fellow practitioner for support. She came to my side and served me the treatment that was downloaded into my mind that morning.

It was my most challenging ceremony to date, but it was the one that truly integrated my deep understanding of the metaphysical anatomy of the spine.

Upon returning to Ali's office a few days later she asked, "What did you do?"

Immediately fearful of what she might report as she was analyzing my spine I asked, "What do you mean?"

She replied, "Your spine is fully back in alignment... I've never seen anything like this before."

Relief washed over my body. I was okay. I was safe. My spine was back in alignment.

It was there in that office I knew I had experienced a medical miracle and I would never underestimate my body's ability to heal itself. I also vowed I would never ignore the signs and symptoms that the body would use to communicate with me ever again.

As I write you now I am presently walking in my life with more alignment than ever before. My spine and back have remained healed and strong and I do not have to seek treatments to manage any symptoms of scoliosis as I simply do not have scoliosis anymore.

The body is always communicating with us and the sooner we open our minds and hearts to receive these messages the faster we can find relief and alignment in our lives.

It's not always easy to face what journey of embodiment, but I promise you it is worth every fear and every fear.

Liberation of the body is liberation of the mind and spirit. May you always choose to listen with love rather than fall victim to the fear of old stories.

You were born a warrior with the power to heal yourself.

~ Zoey Poulsen

An Entry from My Mother

When I was a child my father would frequently move past that of physically disciplining us children and into being severely, verbally abusive towards us. He'd ridicule or call us names, put us down, etc. for one reason or another. My mother was aware of this and often present for it but she never stood up for us kids the way I thought she should and wish she had done so many times. It wasn't until I was an adult that I learned more about my mother and how she was treated as a child, by her grandparents and mother. She became invisible as a preschooler to survive and continued throughout her marriage to be invisible even when her children needed her. The abuse she sustained from her family as a child, stayed with her all her life. This explains why she didn't stand up for us as children, she didn't know how.

My father never left her nor would he have let her leave him and I think that was security for her after not being wanted as a child. Honestly, though, how would have she supported herself and a bunch of kids in the 1950s as a single woman without having many rights at that time? If she left my father, she didn't have a family to turn to, so the sense of security caused her to stay. My father's father and grandfather were also abusive towards my father, so the way my father treated us was how he was treated as a child, he didn't know any other way to be. Both of my parents having been abused as children affected how they were as parents towards myself and my siblings.

I was seven the first time I stood up to my father. I told him that was the last time he would ever lay a hand on me or I would make him sorry. Of course, he laughed at me, as I stood there holding a mop over my shoulder threatening to hit him with it, but it worked, he never laid a hand on me again. The verbal abuse, however, did not stop, he remained verbally abusive for most of his life.

In fact, I have often thought that bones and bruises heal and are forgotten but harmful words are recalled over and over and therefore the hurt is also recalled. There is no truth in the children's jingle, "Sticks and stones will break my bones but words will never hurt me."

I mentioned how my mother became invisible as a child but even not knowing that about her I did the same, picking up this pattern from her. "Out of sight, out of mind" worked when it came to my father. Survival skills at their best.

In my first marriage, I married an abusive person and left him within months because the abuse escalated so quickly, we were divorced before the first year of marriage ended. He was my high school boyfriend and had abused me then, even at the school.

My mother went to the school to file a complaint on my behalf but since he was an important athlete the principal expelled me to end the problem. My mother then went to the school board next to get me re-enrolled, they let me return to school but did not address his behavior. Even after I divorced him, he stalked me and tried to find me for the next 40 years, until he died homeless.

I didn't know who my next husband would be but I knew he was guilty before I met him. Upon deciding to not make the same mistake twice, I read an American advice column titled "Dear Abby" which recommended you sleep on your fiancés's family's couch for one month to see if you are compatible before getting married. Living in different states kept me from sleeping on their couch for a month but over the next couple of years his parents and siblings came to visit and slept on my couch and I slept on theirs when visiting them. I watched them like it was a science experiment and was very surprised to find a family that loved, supported and sincerely cared for their immediate and extended family. I wanted a loving and caring father for our children and to break the cycle in my first marriage and can honestly say after 50 years of marriage to my second husband, I was successful.

After being married to my second husband for over ten years and giving birth to our two daughters, my father came to visit me when I was in my forties, he apologized and asked for forgiveness for his behavior when I was a child. This was the first time he hugged me and told me he loved me. I chose to forgive him because God had been dealing with me about the importance of forgiveness so I listened to that intuition and forgave my father. Forgiveness is a process that can be painful but in time is freeing. Some of my siblings chose to forgive him, while some did not.

I remind myself often of a part of the Lord's Prayer about forgiveness:

Matthew 6:12-14 (New International Version)
12 And forgive us our debts,
as we also have forgiven our debtors.
13 And lead us not into temptation, [a]
but deliver us from the evil one. [b] '
14 For if you forgive other people when they sin
against you, your heavenly Father will also forgive you.

I feel we can reverse the generational curse of abuse by taking God at his word. His word is true, and He has set us free from the curse! When we forgive others we allow for space in our heart for God to do powerful work in breaking generational cycles.

~ Beanie

CLOSNIG THOUGHTS

As you read these stories you can see how forgiveness can come in layers and can take years to come to fruition. When the body is holding the memory of the psyche and an abusive situation, it will hold on to it for as long as you let it. When we take time to slow down, to listen to the self, and to not fear solitude in order to be able to listen, the spirit will always speak louder than the body & mind in order for us to find forgiveness and peace.

Coming back to the concept that we are all having experiences through life that occur in order for us to each come back to a full place of self-love, therefore more love and compassion for those around us. I always like to stress that this isn't an excuse of the poor behavior of one who doesn't do any work on themselves, but it's about forgiving them for your own sanity and healing.

There's a saying about forgiveness that I love, *"Not forgiving someone, is the same as drinking poison and expecting the other person to die."*

In other words, if you have unforgiveness towards someone who's wronged you then that's your choice, it doesn't affect them one bit. Most abusers couldn't care less whether you forgive them or not because from their perspective they are right. Sometimes like in the case of my grandfather someone who's abused you will come back to apologize, this is only after they have done years of extensive work on themselves. In his particular case he was a changed person through his religious beliefs, he spent the later years of his life working in the prison system in Texas as a minister teaching forgiveness to hardened criminals and its value in healing the spirit.

Though I didn't get along with my grandfather for most of my life, he did teach some valuable lessons to his grandkids. I believe that his ministry in the prison system helped to heal him a little bit by a little bit over time. He taught us that people can change when they want to, but they have to want to and they have to be willing to humble themselves. This is a similar philosophy to any Addict program, be willing to admit and apologize for your wrongdoings towards others in order to make deep change within yourself. This is the part of taking responsibility for yourself, not expecting or controlling the outcome but only doing your own work.

I say that people can change though not as an encouragement to try to get someone to change or to wait around hoping they will. This change may never happen for them within this lifetime and will only happen if they want it. I say this as an encouragement to you. You can change your pattern by healing yourself and shifting your perspective. Your body, mind, DNA, and environment are holding on to stories and patterns that are no longer serving you. Like myself when we choose to leave one of these relationships or go no contact with family members this is a bold and powerful but painful step. Without doing more internal work, this is, however, only step one to the healing journey.

I took step one, then needed to go deeper in order to fully stop myself from repeating the pattern. I had to be willing to admit where I was wrong, how badly I'd been hurt, and that I needed deeper healing. My deepest healing has come after being in Bali and doing very deep work on myself in order to forgive. When the spirit of my grandfather appeared to me in a dream, within the dream I got angry that he came to my space, because I hadn't forgiven him. Then he sat down, took off his white cowboy hat that he always wore, and asked for my forgiveness. In my dream state, I immediately calmed down and asked myself, "Why are you holding on to un-forgiveness? Here he is asking for what you've been working towards." In my dream, I sat there staring at him for a few minutes before feeling and truly releasing the anger, and then honestly forgiving him. Not just saying the words to appease the situation but letting it go, and allowing myself to feel this deep sense of relief for what I'd been holding on to for so many years, and potentially in my DNA from my mom or grandmother.

Following this dream, I got sick for three weeks and completely lost my voice for two weeks. I'd never experienced this before, at this level, but I felt the message from my body was releasing where I'd been holding on to that un-forgiveness, in my throat, in my voice. As my book began to pour out of me slowly my voice returned and my spirit lifted, I felt like a whole new woman, and still months into writing this book, I feel wildly fresh.

When you get to your phase of forgiveness don't hesitate, allow yourself to forgive to the depth with which you have at that moment. There's no need for more and certainly no need for you to force yourself, if you're not ready to forgive then don't. That will be your sign that there's something deeper to work on that hasn't yet emerged for you to know what it is. Allow yourself the grief, the anger, the rage, the pain, for through these emotions will release the hurt your body and mind are holding on to and make way for your spirit to emerge. The body and mind have been protecting you from ever getting hurt again, so thank them for holding you in whatever space you are in, and gently move into the next space that you can hold for yourself.

Like Nikki's podcast, you are an Emotional Badass; like Zoey says at the end of each Kambo session, "You are a warrior doing powerful work"; and like my mother, you can forgive and teach your children new ways of being. Like I've said to every client and myself, You fucking got this! You can leave abusive patterns, you can change your stars and you can emerge into a light that's brighter when you've cleared out your karma story. When the journey feels long and the emotions are running high, clench your fists (this is a way to gently release anger), and take a few deep breaths to remind yourself:

"I fucking got this! I am making space to breathe."

~ with love & gratitude,

Johnna

***

A WAY TO BEGIN FINDING FORGIVENESS:

There is a prayer in the Hawaiian culture called, Ho'opono-pono. This ancient practice function as a communication tool for reconciliation, and a tool for restoring self-love and balance. This is a practice that you can do when you feel ready to sit with the emotions of forgiveness and work through the many layers that potentially could come up.

If there's a person or situation, or even a thought pattern that's within you, that you feel needs acceptance and forgiveness, then this prayer is something that can help you to get there.

It's ideal to sit quietly, visualize, or think about the person or situation. See it in front of you with your eyes closed. Then you begin by repeating these four phrases over and over, until you feel compete in this sitting. Emotions will arise, I encourage you to let them come, observe them, and keep repeating the phrase.

I'm sorry
Please forgive me
Thank you
I love you

The intention of chanting these words over and over is to clear the mind, body, and spirit of ill will, shame, guilt, resentment, anger, and hurt. You're not erasing any wrong-doing on your part, rather teaching yourself to hold space for your emotions, and clearing negative energy. We are human and will remember the harmful things done towards us, or that we've done towards others, but the energy can be cleared to where you can accept the lesson.

And learn to love yourself through it.